SOAPROCK COAST
The origins of English porcelain
by Robert Felce

First edition 2011

Published by Robert Felce BSc(Hons)
Riviera Close, Mullion, Cornwall TR12 7AW

ISBN 978-0-9569895-0-5
Copyright © Robert Felce 2011

Above photo: Mullion Cove, The Lizard Peninsula, Cornwall 2011

Produced by Westcountry Printing & Publishing, Churchtown, Mullion, Cornwall TR12 7HQ

Soapstone vein outcropping in Mullion Cove

Preface

The story of Soapstone began over a thousand years ago in China but its importance to Cornwall only began in the mid 18th century.

In 1748 Benjamin Lund, a Quaker Merchant and potter living in Bristol, approached a landowner on the Lizard Peninsula and sought permission to quarry and mine the mineral from a location called Gew Graze , more commonly known as "Soapy Cove" one mile north of Kynance.

The mineral, which at the time was only available in Cornwall, was to be used to manufacture Porcelain.

During the early years of the 1750s a number of other potters including Nicholas Crisp and John Sanders, Richard Chaffers, and Philip Christian made their way to the Lizard in a similar venture. They came from London, Worcester, Liverpool, Shropshire and South Wales.

One of the factories, Worcester, was initially run by a group of 15 Directors including Dr John Wall, Richard Holdship and William Davis, and went on to produce porcelain for over 200 years, becoming one of the most successful businesses ever to operate in this Country.

It began with soapstone from the Lizard Peninsula.

Richard Chaffers, in his quest for soapstone is reported to have ridden the length of the country from Liverpool to London and then to Mullion with a thousand pounds and two pistols in his saddlebags. He went on to locate enough soapstone to start a porcelain factory in Liverpool with Richard Podmore and to draw praise for the quality of his work from no less a potter than Josiah Wedgwood.

There have been books written about the skills of the potters and their pots but very little information has ever been published about the quarrying and mining of the soapstone on the Lizard.

The story and the Industrial and social legacy it left has gone almost unnoticed for over 180 years, almost being totally forgotten.

The products of the English porcelain industry, starting with soapstone from The Lizard, have contributed to the daily lives of every household in this country and many other parts of the world for the last 260 years.

My research has revealed a lost Industrial landscape on the Lizard peninsula and changed the way in which the landscape is interpreted.

This book is an attempt to return the story of soapstone to public awareness, and help teach people a little about the lives of the potters, quarrymen, miners and the people of Mullion and the surrounding countryside over 250 years ago.

In the words of the motto of the Old Cornwall Society "Cuntelleugh an brewyon us gesys no vo kellys travyth".... "Gather ye the fragments that are left, that nothing be lost".

RF

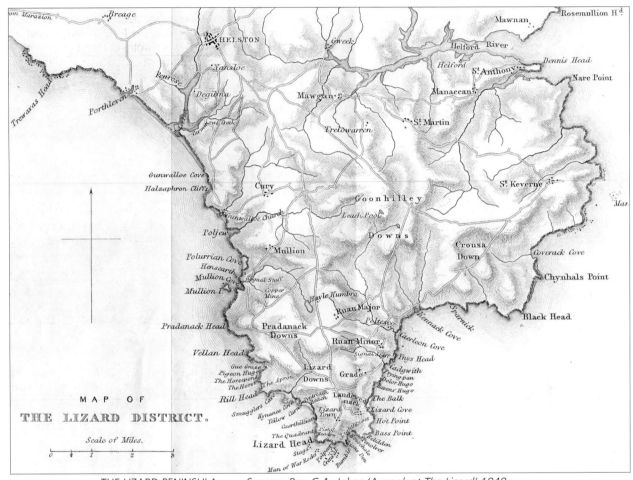

MAP OF
THE LIZARD DISTRICT.

Scale of Miles.

THE LIZARD PENINSULA   *Source: Rev. C.A. Johns 'A week at The Lizard' 1848*

Acknowledgments

There are many people who have provided help and guidance in the preparation of this book which was written over a period of more than 8 months. It is not easy to write about a subject where so little information is in the public domain and for that reason I wish to thank the staff at Truro Record Office, and Angela Broome at the Courtney Library in Truro for digging out the few known academic articles from shelves and drawers. I'd like to thank Sonia Parkinson who wrote academic articles in the 1990's and having gone into retirement, or so she thought, has gone on to advise me about those early academic pieces.

I would also like to thank Paul Holden M.A. at Lanhydrock for his information and helpful e- mails.

The Worcester Porcelain Museum is a great store of wonderful early porcelain. Wendy Cook (who does like Cornish Chocolate) has been a unique provider of information, allowing access to the archive material. Thanks also to Ken Russell for allowing me to watch his immaculate gilding skills at the museum.

Also the North Worcester Archaeological Group (NWAG), especially Francesca Llewellyn who jointly assisted me rooting through the Worcester archives, and Rod Sproat and colleagues who located an important soapstone Licence and dug into the background of Astley Forge Mill.

There's also Malcolm and Joss at the Post Office, who were the first family to view Torchlight Cave "Mine" in the Cove and see it in a new light, as well as Chris Bray for taking time out. Hope all the cuts & bruises have healed. Thanks to Richard Williams at Poldark Mine for his advice on early mining techniques, Janet Spargo at Helston Museum, Mary Vyvyan and the owners at Merthen Quay who kindly allowed me to visit.

Thanks also to Paula Gray at Pentreath Porcelain who introduced me to the quarries at Caerthillian and Pentreath and as far as I know makes the only Porcelain produced on the peninsula in Lizard Village.

There are some people, like Rex Bray of Mullion, who deserve extra thanks for helping to answer nearly all the Cornish questions I put to him, and if he didnt know he would try and find out the answer, and his wife Rosemary who provided tea and cake for weeks on end.... yes it's all nice Rosemary.

Then there are the Mullion Fishermen, Barry Mundy, Jeff Mayer, John Pascoe, and Jeff Rosvear who know more than anyone about the coast, and Mike Anderton who, along with Vic led me in the direction of the old jetty. Also there is Oscar Hill who loves the mining history of his village.

I'd like to say thank you to Peter Starling from the Caughley Porcelain Society, who has boundless enthusiasm for his subject and for his donation of porcelain and photographs of Caughley porcelain.

Thanks also to other private collectors who have generously donated photographs of porcelain shown on the cover and centre pages.

Also, some of the Mullion elders who have provided stories and artifacts from the quarrying era. Then there is Vic the printer, the guardian of Gew Graze, for his help with the project and who now sees soapstone every time he goes to the beach.... and the porcelain potters and miners who started the story over 260 years ago.

Last but by no means least my wife who has put up with all the hassle and made lots of tea, and "Copper" who has accompanied me on the trips up and down all the cliffs, over the Downs and on the beaches.... and been in the picture on lots of photographs. I hope that I haven't forgotten anybody.

RF

Contents

Soapstone Quarry and location of Drift A

Mullion Cliff

Site of Drift B

Porth Pyg Quarry with visible soapstone veins

Ledge B

Entrance to Torchlight Cave (Soapstone Mine)

Tonkens Point (Laden Ceyn)

The Vro

Sandy Vro

Horizontal Drift cut through serpentine promontory to Sandy Vro at beach level.

Perpendicular drive into sloping soapstone vein at beach level.

Start of Ledge A

Perpendicular drive into sloping soapstone vein at beach level.

Henscath Cliff

Drift partially cut into serpentine promontory to remove soapstone.

Drift cut through serpentine promontory removing soapstone and forming cave through to Cove.

SOAPSTONE WORKING AT MULLION COVE

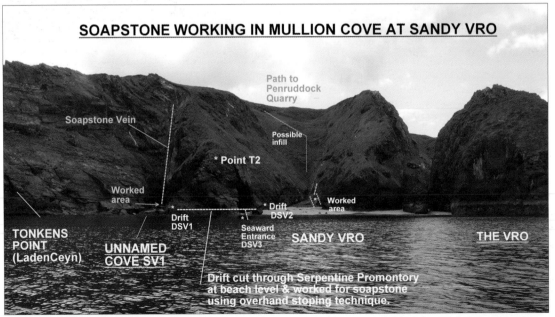

SOAPSTONE WORKING IN MULLION COVE AT SANDY VRO

Soapstone Vein

Path to Penruddock Quarry

Possible infill

* Point T2

Worked area

Worked area

* Drift DSV2

Drift DSV1

* Seaward Entrance DSV3

TONKENS POINT (LadenCeyn)

UNNAMED COVE SV1

SANDY VRO

THE VRO

Drift cut through Serpentine Promontory at beach level & worked for soapstone using overhand stoping technique.

1. Introduction

The Lizard Peninsula is part of the Meneage district of South West Cornwall, and has been described as a place apart where the combination of a mild climate and complex geology has produced an area with a very distinctive character. Historically, one of the most frequently visited areas is the 5 miles of coastline between Mullion Village and Lizard Point. This includes, Mullion Cliff, Predannack, Ogo Dour, Vellan Head, Gew Graze (or Soapy Cove as it is more commonly known), Kynance Cove, much lauded for its beautiful beach, Pentreath and Caerthillian,with its summer flowers but limited access. In common with much of this southern portion of the Lizard Peninsula it is predominantly formed from Serpentine, a derivative of olivine or peridotite, and a rock more usually found deep beneath the oceanic crust. It is a magnesium iron silicate,usually green or red in colour with a waxy or resinous lustre which is still quarried as an ornamental stone and turned on a lathe to produce household ornaments. Often associated with the Serpentine is a soft rock called Soapstone or Steatite, also of metamorphic origin. It frequently occurs in veins or lodes, is rich in the mineral talc and over the years has been subjected to the weathering processes including the rain which drains from the flat plateau of the Lizard Downs.

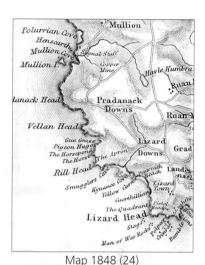

Map 1848 (24)

An example of the earliest English soapstone porcelain

The Southern section of the Lizard Peninsula is part of the Lizard National Nature Reserve and of special importance are the coastal areas from Mullion to Predannack Cliffs and from Vellan Head to Lizard Point. These areas are managed by Natural England, in partnership with many local farmers. In between these 2 sites the coast is managed by the National Trust. The characteristic coastal and heath landscape is recognised as being of national importance as part of the Cornwall Area of Outstanding Natural Beauty. (AONB) Cornwall Wildlife Trust own 2 nature reserves on the Lizard, North Predannack Downs Nature Reserve, gifted to the Trust in 1986, and the Windmill Farm Nature Reserve, purchased in 2001 with the assistance of the Heritage Lottery Fund.(1)

Anyone walking this section of the coast today might be forgiven for believing that the land is a totally natural landscape, but in truth it is an ancient landscape and one which hides the scars of a more recent important industrial age dating back to the 18th century and lasting over 80 years.

The Parish of Mullion covers an area stretching from Cury to the North, to Kynance in the south and includes Mullion Village, and Predannack. In 1875 "it covered 4786 acres, 1700 of which were arable, 1200 were pasture and the rest were commons,crofts and public roads". It contained a number of small agricultural hamlets such as Trewoon, Claher, Trembel and Meaver, and two sites, Garro and Trenance, which were recorded in the Domesday Book.(2)

There are also ancient sites, where burial chambers or barrows have been located. These sites were commonly recorded on earlier maps as "tumuli". The earliest settlement studied in detail is that at Kynance Gate which was occupied on the edge of sloping moorland above a stream running into a rocky valley above Kynance Cove about 1200BC in the Middle Bronze Age. It lies close to a prominent outcrop of Serpentine.

It was subsequently abandoned and later re occupied in the Iron Age through to the Roman period. A number of stone built roundhouses have been discovered in two separate locations.(3)

In November 1871 a group of academics and clergy including Rev. Edmund Harvey investigated a tumulus or burial mound at Predannack situated, *"from the Downs to Hervan Lane on its southern side"*.(4) In a book entitled "Naenia Cornubuiae" written by the Cornish antiquarian William Copeland Borlase (1848-1899), he wrote that, *"The "tumulus" was about 4 foot in height and had a diameter of forty two feet. It was surrounded by a ring of stones set on edge, but otherwise was composed entirely of earth. At a depth of 3 foot the pick axe struck into a substance much harder than the rest of the mound. This turned out to be a bed of white clay common to the country around which was artificially heaped up as a protection to a quantity of calcined bones and ashes.... originally contained in a small urn.... carelessly baked but ornamented with a chevron pattern."*(4a)

This clay was soapstone and it is believed that the reference indicates that it was known to, and may have been used by people living on the Lizard as far back as the Bronze Age, over 3000 years ago.

Many people may be aware that Soapstone or Soap Rock as it was called in the 18th century was quarried at Gew Graze, and they will know the location as "Soapy Cove". It is a small valley 1 mile north of Kynance and west of Windmill Farm Nature Reserve, accessible only from Kynance Cove in the south or from Windy Ridge Farm at Predannack Woollas in the North. What may not be known is the extent of the mining or quarrying activity which took place along this coastal stretch, from Mullion Cove in the north to Caerthillian in the south, and its importance to an embryonic British Porcelain industry. Knowledge of the quarrying and mining has so far been limited to examination of Licences or Indentures issued by Land Owners to the Porcelain potters who were responsible for, and carried out the work to remove the soapstone. A number of the Licences have become available over the years but because some have remained unpublished or lost the whole picture still cannot be painted.

In the 1740's the early industry was trying hard to compete with the seafaring European traders monopolising a Chinese market which had been making stylish and durable porcelain for a thousand years or more, as well as the developing porcelain factories of Europe in Germany, Italy, France and Russia.

2. Soapstone

The Lizard Soapstone, historically known as "Soaprock" because of its soapy feel, consists mineralogically of a cordierite steatite, derived from the alteration of the Lizard serpentine. It has a high magnesium content. In geological and pottery circles today it is called a "Talc" but is often erroneously associated with China Clay which is a derivative of Granite. Although early British geologists such as William Borlase (1696-1772) recorded descriptions of more than 10 types of soapstone,(5) in economic terms there were 4 main types of interest to the potters. The most sought after within the early Porcelain Industry was White. It had a smooth surface, and a soapy or waxy texture. Second in importance was Pale greenish grey,(2% iron) very soapy to touch and with a slightly granular texture. This is the most common. Thirdly was Grey to sage green, (3% iron), could be used in small quantities to augment the soapstone content and fourth was Pink through buff to russet. (4% iron). This was almost unusable. Under analysis the composition, although slightly variable is as follows;

SiO_2 46%, (Quartz)
MgO 43%,
(Magnesium Oxide, or Magnesia. Historically known as Magnesia Alba)
Al_2O_3 8%, (Aluminium Oxide)
Fe_2O_3 2% (Variable),(Ferric Oxide)
CaO 1%, (Calcium Oxide)
H_2O 10% (Water) The Ferric Oxide varies in amount from 0.8%-4%

Gew Graze 'Soapy Cove'

The earliest formula for steatitic porcelain was believed to use as much as 40% soapstone, but this could be reduced to under 30% depending on the other types of clay and other materials used in the mixture but it is the magnesium content which helps provide porcelain with its heat resistant qualities.(5a)

In 1811 the Geologist J.F. Berger wrote, *".... by soaprock is meant a type of steatite, so tender that it may be cut as easily as new cheese. It is embedded in the serpentine. Its colour is pearly white or grey with red and blue veins, and when pure it has a sort of semi transparence. On coming out of the quarry, it may be kneaded like a lump of dough, but after having been exposed to the air for some time, it becomes friable, owing, no doubt, to the evaporation of the great quantity of water it contains, it possesses the soapy feel in the highest degree, and pieces of hard stone are included in it, in pretty large quantity. It is used in the manufacture of porcelain for the same purpose as the kaolin, and on many accounts it might be said that the soaprock is to serpentine, what kaolin is to granite."*(6)

Soapstone specimens from the west coast of The Lizard peninsula

3. What is porcelain?

In order to understand the porcelain industry it is helpful to be aware of the differences between the different types of porcelain.

a) Soft Paste Porcelain. A type of soft paste porcelain was first produced in Europe in 1738 Soft paste porcelain is made from a combination of fine white clay and frit (A mixture of white sand,gypsum,soda, salt, alum and nitre), soapstone or bone ash. Lime and chalk were used to fuse the white clay and the frit, which is then fired at a temperature lower than hard paste porcelain. This allowed it to be decorated using a wider variety of colours. It is translucent but may have an inconsistent patchy appearance. When chipped it has a granular appearance rather than a glassy appearance and may exhibit fire-cracks. The glaze does not fuse with the body as in hard paste, but remains on the surface often allowing it to exhibit crazing. It is less resilient than hard paste and the glaze scratches more easily. Due to production issues, costs, and other shortcomings in comparison to the production of hard paste Porcelain, once the formula for making hard paste porcelain became widely known the manufacture of soft paste was dropped and had mostly ended by the first quarter of the 19th Century.

b) Hard Paste Porcelain. The formula to make hard paste porcelain consists of two main ingredients, China Clay (Kaolin) and China stone (Petuntse). The use of China stone dispenses with the need for frit, used in soft paste porcelain. Both are decomposed forms of granite. This type of porcelain often has a grey appearance and is extremely hard. It is fired at a much higher temperature (1350-1400 degrees C), than soft paste porcelain and actual bonding of clay particles occurs which vitrifies the body to a glass like consistency. It is distinguished by its translucency (allows bright light to pass through) , impermeability and a resonant sound when tapped. It has a brittle structure and if broken has a tendency to shatter into glassy fragments rather than rough chunks or pieces like pottery.

c) Bone China This type of Porcelain is similar to hard paste porcelain but contains 45% to 50% of bone ash, which gives it the ivory white appearance. It also contains china clay and china stone. The standard formula is 25% china clay, 25% Cornish Stone, 50% bone ash. It was first made in England about 1795-1797, the body of bone china is very strong, white translucent and resistant to thermal shock. It is also easier to manufacture. Josiah Spode introduced his new bone china pottery on 1797, and was the best solution to the quest for Porcelain. Technically it was a hard paste porcelain because it is a mixture of clay and another non glassy material.

Bone China became the English porcelain because it is less liable to loss in firing than soft paste porcelains which contain glass. The firing temperature is much lower (1240 degrees C) than for hard paste porcelain (1400 degrees C) allowing the potters to use their existing ovens. In the late 18th century and early 19th century the Government had placed high import duties on porcelain and merchant trading vessels were reduced in order to help sustain naval and military forces abroad.(7)

4. "… for all the tea in China"

The Chinese invented porcelain over a thousand years ago in the Tang Dynasty (618-906 A.D.) but the formula was a closely guarded secret. In 1279 Kublai Khan, the Mongol tribal leader invaded China and with it created an empire covering Korea, China, Central Asia, to the Middle East and Europe stretching westwards to the Danube and the Adriatic Sea. Within this empire all earlier trade barriers were removed and scientific discoveries were exchanged. Missionaries, diplomats and traders were lured to China by easier travel which included the reopening of the legendary Silk Route. In the 13th Century Marco Polo returned from the Court of Kublai Khan with, amongst other things the first examples of Chinese Porcelain ever seen in the west, calling it "porcellane". In the 14th and 15th Centuries it became a prized possession, often being encased in gold and silver mountings because it was so rare. Because of the dominance of the Arabs at this time on the sea routes leading to the far East, trading became more difficult but gradually explorers such as Columbus and the Portugese Vasco da Gama reached the far east initially via India and created new links for trade with China. By the 16th Century the Portugese were trading closely with the Chinese markets and were to be the first to import Porcelain to Europe. By 1522 shipments of blue and white porcelain amounting to 40-60,000 pieces came into Portugal every year. The Spanish joined the trade with China but they took a different route, avoiding the Portugese, with trading goods being shipped from China to the Philippines and Mexico,crossing Mexico by land and then returning across the Atlantic, thus avoiding conflict. In England Queen Elizabeth the First owned as many as 1500 pieces of Porcelain, much of it brought back by Sir Francis Drake. In 1600 she presented the London East India Company with a Royal Charter but it was not until 1643 that the English were granted trading concessions by the Chinese.

The Dutch East India Company was formed in 1602 for the sole purpose of trading with China, but they also plundered the Portugese boats returning from China, taking their vessels and thousands of pieces of porcelain cargo back to Amsterdam where they renamed it "kraakporselein" or "kraak". In the 1600s there were changes in the way China was governed with war preoccupying the country, but that change allowed the Chinese potters artistic freedom and a wider variety and decoration and style of porcelain was produced. There were special orders of porcelain covering millions of pieces being transported to Europe, and porcelain became a major factor in world trade.

England began to develop a monopoly of trade with the Far East, and although the demand was mainly for tea, it brought a demand for the items of porcelain used to make and drink it. It was the Portugese and the Dutch who first imported tea in the 1650s, but in fact it was Catherine of Braganza, the Portugese wife of Charles II who encouraged its consumption in England from 1662. The traders brought strange pots with spouts, and cups and saucers of white porcelain, or fine hard red pottery, and for most British consumers they looked like nothing they had seen before. Their delicacy and the whiteness and the translucency of porcelain put them in a different class from the relatively coarse British pots. The only viable alternative material was silver. To those with money it provided them with an opportunity to show off their wealth and taste, with glamorous imported porcelain and many would have their portraits painted drinking tea, as a sign of gracious living. It was only the Chinese porcelain which could withstand the high temperatures and boiling water required to make these drinks. English produced products cracked and broke under the stress of thermal shock rendering them unfit for such use. Coffee houses preceded the tea houses in London and liquid and dry tea was being supplied to the public by 1657 but at £6 and £10 per pound was expensive to say the least. As tea drinking became more popular so the price fell. In 1698 the Government decided to put a Tax on tea, encouraged by the brewers who were losing revenue. By 1700 there were 500 coffee houses also selling tea, and by 1750 tea was so popular that it had become the favoured drink of Britains lower classes.. By 1765 it was estimated that 9 out of 10 families in Britain drank tea twice a day.(10) Although expensive it was obtainable by the working classes, largely due to the smuggling trade which was operating on an enormous scale.(8)

Between 1770-1783 5.8 million pounds of tea was imported annually into Britain, but almost the same amount was smuggled illegally, with Cornwall and Devon high on the list for smuggling. In 1753 William Borlase wrote that,"*The coasts here swarm with smugglers from the Lands End to the Lizard....*".(9) It was so organised that armed ships of 300 tons and manned by up to 100 men were used for smuggling. They could make 7 or 8 voyages per year bringing in as a part of their illicit cargo 10-12 tons of tea at a time.

In 1757 William Cutler broke open the customs warehouse at Penzance and stole 15 bags of tea for which he was caught and sentenced to 7 years transportation.(10)

One man told how in 1765 his servants had unloaded a legal cargo and travelled overnight across the moors where they met smugglers with 60 horses, each loaded

Porcelain owned by Queen Elizabeth 1 (8)

with 3 bags of tea weighing about 56lbs each which had been unloaded from a ship earlier that night and were en route to Devon.(11)

In 1784 the Prime Minister William Pitt removed the Tax on Tea with the Commutation Act, reducing the tax from 119% to 12.5%, recognising that it was now established as a national drink.(12) By 1830 the annual consumption of tea had risen to 30 million pounds by weight, and by 1836 annual consumption stood at 49 million pounds. During the 18th Century millions of pieces of Porcelain were shipped from China to Europe. It became essential that Britain was able to manufacture its own Porcelain… and in enormous quantities.

5. A "potted" history of early English and European porcelain

In the 17th and 18th Centuries scientific and practical experimentation was a slow, sporadic and expensive process in Europe, with new methods of manufacture and new materials being sought. New techniques, new kilns, and new methods of production were investigated, and invented. Wastage was high, and modern archaeological digs at the sites of old potteries at that time have revealed millions of sherds of wasted pottery. About 1645 the Royal Society (The National Academy of Science) was set up in London as an "invisible college of natural philosophers", and its activities involved weekly meetings of some of the countries foremost scientists of that time. Their aim was to acquire knowledge by observation and experimental investigation,…. now called "Science", but their efforts were often thwarted by civil war and an unstable society. The group continued to meet at Gresham College until 1658 when they had to disband in fear of their lives as soldiers took over their meeting rooms and London underwent a period of terror. The Society did not fully resume their activities until 1660 with the return of King Charles II when there was an inaugural meeting of 12 eminent men, which included Christopher Wren, Robert Boyle and John Wilkins, Robert Moray and Viscount Bruckner. The King was approached and gave his approval for the Society to continue. This number later grew to 52 and in 1662 King Charles II, granted the Society a Royal Charter.(13)

Although interested in the widest range of experimentation and improvement of knowledge from an early stage, the Royal Society did show an interest in helping develop a porcelain industry in the Country. Names associated with the society included Hans Sloane, founder of the British Museum and the man who brought Drinking Chocolate Milk from the West Indies, the chemist and physicist Robert Boyle, Robert Hooke (The first curator of experiments), Christian Huygens,William Oliver, born in Ludgvan, Cornwall and who was a relative of another Cornishman Dr William Borlase, Alexander Pope , Christopher Wren, and Isaac Newton.

In 1667 a sample of the "soapyrock" from The Lizard was presented by Dr Pope for testing by Robert Boyle (14) and in 1681 it was included by Nehemiah Grew (1641-1712) as "soapstone,steatites" in his "Catalogue and Description of the Natural and Artificial Rarities belonging to the Royal Society".

In 1671 an English potter called John Dwight working in Fulham took out a patent for "transparent earthenware commonly knowne by the name porcelaine or china" and "stoneware vulgarly called Cologne ware" This was not regarded however as true porcelain, but shows an early interest in developing new quality wares. These early potteries were small but intensely competitive.

In the early 18th Century The Royal Society became aware of the existence of the materials used by the Chinese to making porcelain partly through visits to France by Dr. Cromwell Mortimer between 1719 and 1724. (14) Scientific lectures in France attended by Mortimer were given in Latin in order to try and preserve secrecy.

By 1729 Dr John Woodward (1665-1728) claimed in a work presented posthumously to the Royal Society that experiments had been carried out on Cornish Soaprock and proved it to be suitable for the manufacture of porcelain. Information was also passing across the Atlantic from America and shortly after the Society sponsored visits to Carolina and Georgia to examine clays found there which might be suitable for porcelain manufacture. Dr Cromwell Mortimer subsequently became secretary of the Royal Society and he himself was involved in creating a high temperature thermometer and a new type of furnace fuelled by charcoal. His wind furnace was developed by 1736. The Society was interested in helping to set up a porcelain industry in the Country and were in possession of the materials and methods of manufacture of Oriental Hard Paste Porcelain, English Steatitic Porcelain, English Phosphatic (bone-ash) porcelain and the glassy type of porcelain favoured in France.(15)

How was the secret of Porcelain obtained ? The Chinese, had their well kept secret and Europe was keen to learn. They were also able to produce porcelain with properties which included being able to withstand the temperature of boiling water.

A French Jesuit missionary priest, Pere Francois Xavier Entrecolles, first went to China in 1698. He developed a profound knowledge of the chinese language and took great interest in understanding the Chinese customs. His detailed observations of life in Jingdezhen included the production of high quality porcelain which had been successful for over a thousand years. Jingdezhen was situated on a plain surrounded by high mountains and was the centre of chinese production. Trade was commonplace and even the Japanese came to buy porcelain there. The port on one of the rivers there was over 3 miles in length. Entrecolles wrote that at the time of his arrival there were over 3000 porcelain kilns in Jingdezhen and that the city was a mass of burning furnaces both day and night. Included in the lengthy letter of 1712 was information which identified two essential ingredients for making porcelain. One was called pe-tun-tse and the other kaolin. The former was white,very fine earth and was quarried some miles away from where it was used. The chinese believed that the best material had a greenish tinge. The kaolin, which was mined in the mountains was also white and according to the chinese gave the porcelain strength. Both materials were processed and refined before use and both had to be used in the manufacturing of the porcelain. Entrecolles investigated all the processes involved in the making of the porcelain in great detail, including firing and decoration and glazing of the products.

In a second letter in 1722 Entrecolles wrote that the chinese had recently found a new material as a replacement for kaolin. It was a stone similar to chalk called hoa-che. In use it was broken up and placed in a vat of water to dissolve, and was described by him as being viscous and in a way resembled soap.(16)

There were numerous attempts to produce porcelain in europe, which were based on collections of porcelain from China and Japan, some of which were almost successful. Independently in 1710, and unknown to Entrecolles, a German goldsmith called Johann Freidrich Bottger developed a method of manufacturing hard paste porcelain which led directly to the setting up of the Meissen porcelain factory in the Gothic Albrechtburg castle. He was the first manufacturer of Porcelain in Europe and it was composed of kaolinite, quartz and alabaster fired at a temperature of over 1350 degrees Centigrade. In fact it was reported that it was so secret that few people knew the whole recipe and most only knew part of the recipe. The quality of the porcelain was good but there were problems in the decorating and firing. The secret however did get out and potters set up to compete. They did in fact use Kaolin in the recipe, but they produced soft paste porcelain. A crossed swords mark was introduced in 1720 to protect the identity of the Meissen porcelain and it had developed so well that by 1750 Meissen was employing 700 people. Even as the English industry was developing in the 1750s it was apparent that the Meissen porcelain was competitive and much admired, so much so that its import into this country was severely restricted and was imitated by porcelain manufacturers.

An early form of soft paste porcelain was made in Italy in the 17th Century but it wasn`t until 1720 that Porcelain was again produced in Italy on a large scale. This was in Venice by Francesco Vezzi and was a hard paste porcelain used mainly to manufacture teapots. It closed after 7 years but was followed by other porcelain factories including the Capodimonte factory, established in Naples in 1743 by Charles de Bourbon, who became Charles VII, King of Naples and Sicily. He married Maria Amalia, daughter of the King of Saxony and Grand Daughter of the founder of the Meissen factory in Germany.

In 1727 a French entymologist and physicist called Rene Antoine Ferchault Reaumur, known for developing a working cupola furnace in 1720 and a new thermometer scale in 1731 , also studied the chinese porcelain, and reported to the French Science Academy that he had produced a porcelain similar to that of the chinese. Reaumur had received some samples of the Chinese kaolin and other materials with which he experimented and by 1740 had produced an opaque glass known as Reaumur Porcelain. Unfortunately he could not find their equivalent in France.(17)

6. The early British interest in soapstone

The Rev. William Borlase (1696-1772), was born in the Parish of St. Just, West Cornwall. According to the Ashmolean Museum to which he donated his Collections of minerals and antiquities, he graduated with an M.A. from Exeter College, Oxford in 1719, was ordained as a priest in 1720, and was proposed by Emanuel Mendes da Costa and admitted to the Royal Society in 1750. Borlase concentrated on the natural resources, minerals, religion and antiquities of Cornwall. He devoted a lot of time to the development and understanding of the nature of minerals and this included the possible uses of soapstone. He noted that in 1728 Dr John Woodward an English naturalist, and geologist had written in his book "A Catalogue of Fossils Volume 1" about the Cornish soapy clays at the Lizard as *" being suitable for porcelain manufacture"* Between 1735 and 1738 Borlase had written to several scientists and sent to them samples of the Cornish Soaprock for experimentation. He went on to record in great detail the description, properties and location of soapy clay at Kynance and at Gew Graze.(18)

Emanual Mendes da Costa an English botanist, naturalist and mineralogist was elected as a Fellow of the Royal Society by 1747. Although living in London he travelled widely, recording his observations. From early in 1748 he had exchanged a series of letters with Borlase on the pretext of writing a paper on the properties of soaprock for the Societies Transactions. Borlase referred him to Thomas Frye of Bow, a potter who made London China, in the belief that he may be in possession of better information about the properties of the Soaprock, and there is a small chance that they had it in experimental use at that time.

Da Costa subsequently described in his book, entitled "A natural history of fossils" a variety of Lizard clays and their uses but was particularly keen to point out that *"......... no species of clays, whatever, can be finer or fitter for the making of porcelain than these hardened or talcy soap clays where nature has blended the necessary fossils, talc and clay, ready for our use, I am therefore convinced that these steatite pounded then moistened and worked up like a paste with some proportion of fine soft clay,with due management, would make an elegant porcelain , I recommend the experiment for trials to the manufactories lately established in this kingdom, and should they succeed, I doubt not we shall be able to surpass the manufactures of the other european nations, since none as I can learn have the steatite in such plenty as Cornwall affords us, no so fine."* (19)

How then did these soap clays appear to the travellers of the early 18th Century?

Borlase described in his book published in 1758, many different types of soapstone he found in Gew Graze. This is one of many types of soapstone he described. *"The pure white is a close grained glossy clay, dissolves soon in water, is tasteless, sticks a little to the tongue, deposits a yellow pulpy settlement at the bottom above which a cloud of the finest parts continues suspended; mixed with oil, it becomes greasy, tis also too fat to make a body of colour for painting in water, and makes no effervescence with aqua fortis It is very absorbent and takes spots out of silk, without injuring the colour, and is possibly the same, which Bishop Pontipiddan (18th Century Historian) calls the "white talc-stone" of such whiteness, that it is used in Norway, for powder as it may be pulverised into an impalpable fineness". This is carefully selected, from other sorts of clay, barrelled up and almost wholly engrossed, by people employed under the managers of the porcelain manufactures."*

Aqua fortis is Nitric acid in water and was used for separating silver from gold or copper.

Another type was described as follows; *"A glossy pearl coloured hard clay approaching nearly to the consistence of a white* opaque spar, soon cleaves itself into granules when immersed in water, yet dissolves no farther, but with water grinds soon into a flesh coloured milky pulp, 'tis much harder than soap or wax, saws freely and greasy; there is a more stony variety of this clay and more speckled with purple, so that you can scarce break it with a hammer." Emanuel Mendes Da Costa wrote the following; "....The veins of steatites are of different breadths, some run under the sea, some to near the top of the cliff, and some up through the cliff up into the country, and seem in their course to cross the tin loads. Nearer the Lizard than the soaprock, is another cove called Pintrith, which affords a greyish impure steatites spotted with black. The new soaprock lately discovered is at Gew Grez or Crez Cove in the tenement of Kynas, in Mullion Parish. It is about 3 miles from Mullion town and about a mile from the old soap rock or cove, which lies further southward. The entrance into the creek or cove is very steep craggy and horrid, on the right hand (descending into the creek) the hills are crested with naked rocks or cairns, as the Cornish people call them, the sides have also many, but they are small: about half way down the cove a very small current of water traverses it, in a very serpentine manner, and discharges itself near the load or principal vein of the steatites. On the right hand as you descend the cove it grows more craggy and much narrower and a few yards lower on the same side lies the main vein or load of steatites. The various sorts are blended together in spots, sometimes in greater quantities in one place than in another: in the white and red veined steatites, pieces of a compact hard slightly pellucid sparry substance are frequently found: the main vein or load is about 8 foot over; it does not consist purely of the steatites but also holds quantities of rubble or fragments of a hard smooth dusky greenish, and red coloured talcy like fissile stone called by the inhabitants a variegated killas. Some small pieces of white spar are met with, but rarely. About 200 paces higher, on the left hand I found a very soft and very greasy straw coloured steatites : in the sides of the country, that is of the solid strata that enclose the vein, and intermixed with it, lay a reddish brown steatites, but the straw coloured kind was in the greatest quantity; further down, near the level of the sea, the steatites load has been more regularly traced, and makes a course of about 14 inches wide between regular sides, the left hand side the cove is quite perpendicular, and consists of a hard black stone, seemingly divided into strata by small horizontal fissures, placed at great distances from each other; the other sides of the cove are more open and rugged, the sea beats strongly into the creek, which at low water has a small sandy beach."(19) Thus we have Gew Graze towards the start of the Industrial Revolution through the eyes of Emanuel Mendes Da Costa.

Gew Graze...the narrow valley

Soapstone vein Gew Graze

The 1740s saw an increase in the number of potteries and amongst them were Limehouse and Bow. The production of early porcelain required a great deal of experimentation with the potters suffering many costly failures in the firing. Many early potteries failed through a lack of funding and were always in need of extra finance. Kilns were expensive to run, requiring large amounts of fuel and an accurate means of temperature control. A number of archaeological groups have been able to undertake excavations of old potteries where many thousands of pieces of broken porcelain have been recovered along with evidence of the kilns used.

Modern chemical analysis of the fragments has allowed comparisons to be made which are beginning to identify chronologies, sources of the materials used, the individual potters and the various successes and failures of these potteries. Close examination of archived documents and letters by academics has led to a reclassification of pottery and the potters involved in its manufacture and the factories.

One such investigation has led to information about the Bow factory in London where the proprietors included Thomas Frye and a "sleeping partner" Edward Heylin. Bow was active from about 1747-1764 and a rival of the Chelsea porcelain factory in the manufacture of soft paste porcelain. Thomas Frye was a successful Irish artist and inventor before coming to England in 1734 and developed a method of making soft paste porcelain. One of Heylyns associates at this time was a man called Benjamin Lund.(1692-1768). He was born in Hammersmith, Middlesex and both of his parents were members of the Society of Friends (Quakers). In 1706 he was apprenticed to become a brassfounder and stay maker and in 1714 moved to Bristol setting up his own business as a brass founder.

The port of Bristol, at this time was receiving regular cargoes of copper ore from the copper mines around Camborne and Gwennap. This copper was being smelted in Bristol and at Redbrook on Wye by a fellow Quaker, John Coster, son of a Forest of Dean ironmaster. The raw materials for his trade were therefore near at hand. Lund became known to Coster. In 1719 Lund married Christobel Ingram, late of London, and they moved to Bristol. In 1720 their first child Mary was born, and in 1727 they had a son John. Mary died in 1728 aged 8 years. Lund also experimented with methods of refining copper ores, some of which contained impurities such as arsenic, silver, and iron.

In 1728 Lund finally perfected his copper ore refining process and took out a patent together with Francis Hawksbee, for his method of manufacturing copper and extracting silver from copper. Hawksbee lived in London where he was a physicist, chemist and librarian of the Royal Society. Lund later moved to London and attended meetings of the Quaker Society of Friends and it was there that he met with Edward Heylin, a glass maker who had premises in Bow with a reputation for making good quality flint glass.

Lund lost two more children to disease including smallpox and decided to move back to Bristol with his wife and one son also called Benjamin, living at St Phillips in the Plain. In 1738 his wife bore another child, a son, who only lived for 18 months. While living in London Lund had shown an interest in the making of opaque glass and "semi porcelain" through his association with Heylin. In Bristol, back alongside Heylin he started a pottery business but details of it are sparse. He obtained credit and some financial help from 3 Bristol businessmen but whilst in London had lent money to a man called William Crispe of Chelsea which had not been repaid. Unfortunately one of the three business men from Bristol, Henry Casamajor called in his loan to Lund. At this time Crispe was also made bankrupt and when Lund pressed for his money he found that Crispe could not pay him. Lund was "gazetted" as bankrupt even though it was shown that he was owed money himself. Lund then returned to St Giles in the Fields in London where several of the Quaker Society of Friends, in particular the Heylyns, helped him make a new start.

In 1741 Lunds son was apprenticed to a butcher Edward Kibble at Lambeth, who also had connections in the pottery industry. In 1744 Edward Heylin went into partnership with Thomas Frye, the Irish Quaker, to start up the Bow China factory where Lund was now believed to be a workman. Whilst there an American Quaker brought them samples of a kaolin like material from Virginia called "Unaker" clay. Much of their early experimental work was done with this clay at the Heylin glasshouse, and from it they produced a soft paste porcelain made from this clay, glass frit, flint and lime.(5a)(19a)

They were believed to be conversant with French research, such as that of Jean-Baptiste Du Halde who had translated and published an in depth description of the Pere D`Entrocolles letters, (1737) and the requirement for a kaolin like material to make true chinese type porcelain. There were two materials known to be used in China, one was "petuntse", a white kaolin clay and the other material was "wha shee", "Hua Shih" or "slippery stone". Heylin and Frye believed that their "Unaker" or "Cherokee clay" was the true equivalent of the Chinese material described by Du Halde.

In 1745 William Borlase working on the Lizard Peninsula, identified in his writings the existence of a material which he thought was identical to the "wha shee" and sent samples up to London. These were samples of Soaprock.(5)

After a couple of years at Bow, early in 1746 Lund set up a China factory at Dicks Shore, in Limehouse, helped by Jacques Planche, a French potter who went on to work at Longton Hall. The methods and mixtures are not known although Nankin style ware was produced. He advertised the wares in the Daily Advertiser on January 1st 1747 describing it as *"the new invented blue and white Limehouse ware"*, but within a few months of the sale the factory got into financial difficulties and was forced to close. Lund then returned to Bristol, seemingly intent on producing porcelain again he obtained financial backing from the Quaker William Miller, a grocer and baker in St Johns Bristol. Lund sought and found premises at Lowdens Glasshouse at Redcliff Backs.

7. Notes on early life in Mullion

a) Of Cornwall in the 18th Century it was described as *"a wild, inhospitable place, there were few roads and people lived in small towns and hamlets often isolated from each other by many miles. The chief occupations were fishing farming and tin mining."(20d)*

b) In the 18th Century Mullion was still regulated by Manorial Law. A Manor was a parcel of land granted by the King to a Lord or other high ranking person.

In land law, the term *"manor"* does not denote a building, it denotes a system of land management.

It was the right of the Lord to be able to hold a court called the court baron, which was organised to maintain and enforce the services and duties that were owed to the Lord of the Manor. The lands which constituted the manor holdings included tenement lands and demesne lands. The tenement lands were given by the Lord to his followers and retainers in Freehold. Demesne lands were retained for his own use but part to tenents in copyhold.- those who took possession of the land by virtue of the evidence or copy in the records of the Lords court.

A portion of the desmesne lands, called the Lords waste, served as public roads and common pasture land for the Lord and his tenants.

The word Manor also meant the right to receive rents and services from the copyholders.(20e)

These details help explain the setting out of the 1841 Tithe and Apportionment records of Mullion Parish held at Truro Record Office.

Under the Manorial system tenants could not inherit the land, and the Lord of the Manor owed them nothing beyond protection and maintenance. In theory the Lord could seize the land back if a tenant failed to pay rents or services or if no heirs appeared to claim the tenancy after the death of the holder.(20)

Each Manor had its own Court which dealt with among other things,breaches of the *"law of the manor."* The Court had a form of jury composed of 12 local *"Freemen"*, and the entire population of the manor was required to attend each Court and they could be fined for not attending or being represented.

Landowners in Cornwall possessed land over wide areas which was not confined to the immediate vicinity of the Manor House itself, and there were many transfers of ownership during the 18th and 19th Centuries, something which went on, for example, to affect the payments made to landowners by those potters granted Licences to extract Soapstone.

The court *"rolls"* were hand written in book form and in some areas survive today. One such important record does survive for the Manor of Predannack Wartha, in the Mullion Parish and still shows records of attendance from people connected to the period when the extraction of soapstone began, and whose descendents still live in the Village and surrounding area.

Old thatched cottage
Donated by a local resident

In 1750 it was the Law Court of Mary Hunt, then the *"Lady"* of Lanhydrock. It was held on the 8th of October.

The Free Tenants included The Earl of Godolphin, Richard Vyvyan, John St Aubin, Richard Erisay, Viscount Falmouth, William Penrose, Hugh Tonken, Samuel Foot, John Thomas, Anthony Trengrouse, Henry Logidda, Richard Williams, John Shepherd, Christopher Hawkins and Richard Arundle. (15 names of 19 recorded)

The list of Conventionary tenants recorded included the following, Thomas and Peter Thomas, William Hendy, Samuel Trounson, Edward Richards, Oliver Willey, James Harvey, Peter Roberts, Henry Williams, William Tonken, William Mundy, John Sandry, James Harry, John John, John Nicholls, George Hoskens, Elleanor Kellway, Anthony Martyn, John Lakes, Peter Hall, James Millett, John Rapson, Francis Hamblyn, John Bashar, Matthew Wills, George James Kempthorne, Renatus Kempthorne, Robert Roskilly, John James, William Trapling, John Harry, Peter Richards,Mary John, Salomy Courtise, George Jennings, John Lawrence, and Phillippa Mundy. (37 names of 46 recorded)

A copy of the original document is reproduced in Appendix 4.(69)

Many properties and tenancies in rural Cornwall were held under a lease system which was almost peculiar to the County. It was advantageous to the Landowner inasmuch as it helped convert otherwise unusable common, uncultivated or otherwise unusable land to agricultural land, thus allowing a rent to be charged. The system was known as *"A Lease dependent on Lives"*. The system is explained later under sub paragraph (q) but the Manor Courts recorded changes in tenancy and also changes in the Lives record on the Leases which were in existence at the time. For example, the death of all the persons named could result in the tenant being removed from his land and replaced by another tenant. These changes were recorded by hand in the Court Book.

c) The Rev. Luke Tyerman wrote *"Smuggling was considered an honourable traffic, and the plunder of shipwrecked mariners was regarded as a lawful prize. Drunkenness was general and cockfighting, bullbaiting, wrestling and hurling were the favourite amusements of the people"(20d)*

d) It was a time when Cornish people began to receive, and with some initial opposition, accept inspiration from the Methodist Preachers Charles and then John Wesley who were able to preach in the open air to thousands of people, particularly in the Mining districts. On September 7th 1762, two days after he first preached at Gwennap Pit, John Wesley arrived at Mullion on the invitation of Ursula Triggs of Angrouse Farm where he gave a sermon in a field at Parc Venton.

e) Transport by sea was responsible for carrying not only cargoes but also essential information about what was happening in the world and smuggling was a way of life for many in Cornwall, usually involving the so called "Free Trade" with the French.

f) Supplies of food including meat were often limited and when affordable had to be reared at home. Families were large and with little income.

g) The Lizard Peninsula has shallow soil but a favourable climate and was suitable for wheat, barley, oats, turnips and mangolds. Some of these would be required to feed livestock, while cattle were moved between winter and summer grazing to obtain the best grass. Vegetables were early but harvests could be very late.

h) The thatched Cottages built of cob and stone, were often built with a cow shed or barn attached to the one habitable room in the house. Pigs, kept for food, might be some of the only meat eaten by a family if they could afford to feed them. It was said that *"the Cornish people had a use for everything except the squeal"*.(11)

i) Families tended to be large, often with 5 or 6 children and while there would only be one room in the cottage there was room above in the rafters, where the children often slept in a makeshift structure built underneath the thatch called a *"tarfat"*.

j) Fortescue Hitchens wrote in 1824 *"The quality of the land in this parish is generally good especially for grain. On some of the best estates the farmers are in the habit of tilling their wheat in the spring.... 15-20 bushels per acre .... To this fertility the nature of the the soil no doubt contributes, as a little below the surface a species of marl is found, which though hard when discovered, decomposes when exposed to the sun and air and becomes a valuable ingredient in manure. Marl clay and serpentine run throughout the parish but the former and the latter are the most abundant. On the north east part of the parish, in sheltered situations, elm ash and sycamore and apple trees will thrive tolerably well, but on the south west which is exposed to the sea and storms ..... scarcely any tree can be made to flourish."*(20c)

k) There were several grist mills near to the mouth of Mullion Cove, and at Kynance where there was a windmill. These prepared the grain for flour.

l) Mullion, like all other areas of the Cornish Coast relied heavily on the Fishing industry, with pilchards and mackerel forming a staple diet and an income. Although some stocks were sold away from the villages quantities of fish would have to be dried or salted down and preserved to last over the winter. Although the boats were hauled up and the fishing gear maintained on the foreshore at the Cove, a lot of the fishermen lived in the village and would often work on the farms and tenements. However their boats in the Cove would already be loaded ready for work at a minutes notice.

m) Taxes were as unpopular in the 18th century and 19th century as they are now, and were said to be one of the main reasons for smuggling. Items such as Brandy, and Tea were smuggled in huge quantities , and even the essential salt was subject to tax.

n) Fuel for the fires in the thatched cottages came from *"furze"* or gorse allowed to grow especially for the purpose until much later when deliveries of coal were made by passing cargo ships or hauled by cart from Gweek.

o) The farms had large numbers of orchards from which the apples were pressed to make cider for local consumption, the presses often driven by horses. Old Maps show that on most of the farms the valleys were wooded with fruit trees along almost their whole length. In addition to meadows, the valleys and low lying land had willow gardens and plantations which were used to manufacture fishing pots,containers and fences. Both sides of the road leading down to the harbour at Mullion were lined with fruit trees. Nothing was wasted and the people were skilled.

Mullion in the 1750s existed as a group of small agricultural farm cottage groups surrounding the area known as Churchtown built around the ancient St. Mellanus Church. This helped form the triangular core of the village, which it exists today. The Church of St. Melanus was partially rebuilt in 1500 by Robert Luddra. It comprises a chancel, nave & north and south aisles.

p) Population details in the 1750s are not known with the first census information being available in 1801. The population in the 1801 census show that Mullion had 102 habitable houses and 5 uninhabited ones. There were 102 families and a population of 520 ..... an average of over 5 per household. The 1811 census showed a small decrease in the number of houses, but an overall

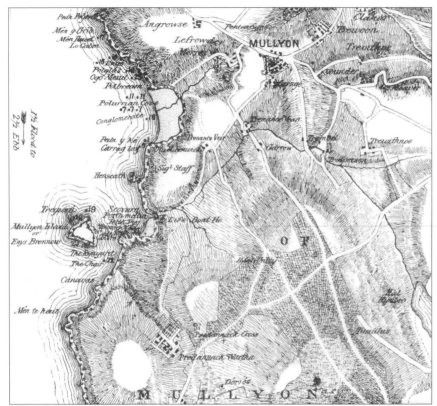

Map reference (24)

Caughley shell dish 18th century
Courtesy Peter Starling

increase in population to 571. The population increased steadily until 1841 when it began to fall.(20c)

q)The farm cottage groups, such as Trewoon, Trenance, Garro, Meaver, Trembel, Vounder and others are now incorporated within the village community, but 250 years ago they would have been separate areas with perhaps 3 to 5 thatched farm cottages located close together near to a spring or stream water supply.

Many cottages, mostly cob and thatch, were held under a system called "A lease dependant on Lives". *"Under such leases a piece of land could be obtained at a nominal rent, and on it the lessee would proceed to erect a house, with the understanding that at the death of the longest lived of three selected persons, the ground, together with all the buildings and improvements effected thereon, should revert to the original owner. The latter might then retain it for his own use, let it or sell it to another, or allow the renewal of the lease to the first tenant under the payment of a "fine". This system was advantageous to the Landowners allowing thousands of acres of waste land to be*

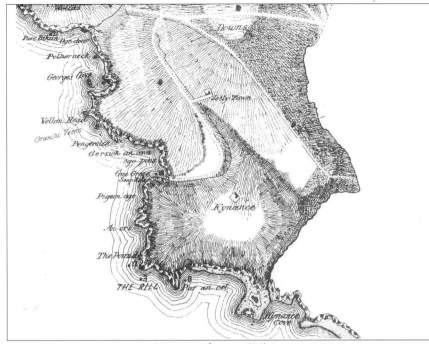

Map reference (24)

Caughley tea canister 18th century
Courtesy Peter Starling

brought under cultivation which would otherwise be unused and possibly unusable even today."(21)

r) It is likely that one of the areas influenced by the quarrying and mining would have been the transport system which would only have consisted of lanes or cart tracks cut into the bedrock or in embedded clay, and locally sourced marl or soil. They would be wide enough for one or occasionally 2 carts.

In October 1758 William Borlase prepared for the government a memorandum on roads in Cornwall entitled "Of the usefulness of, and objections to, Turnpikes in general, and particularly in Cornwall" which was presented to Parliament under an alias, which read *"A great part of their roads is on the hills and open Downs, and these have either no path, or consist of what is worse, a great many deep paths but no formed road"*(22)

A.K. Hamilton Jenkin wrote in "Cornwall and the Cornish" in 1933 that *"It is clear that wheeled traffic continued to be regarded as very much of an innovation in West Cornwall throughout the earlier part of the 18th Century."* and *"In the absence of roads suitable for wheeled traffic, practically the whole of the merchandise of the country districts continued to be carried, until almost the end of the 18th Century, on the backs of mules and ponies, the latter belonging to the little Goonhilly breed".*(23) The situation was helped slightly with the introduction of Turnpike roads but even in 1761 the turnpike-road reached only as far as Marazion and certainly not the Lizard.

s) In Mullion the old "Cove Road" ran from Churchtown, passing Trenance Vean and Garrow which lay to the south, then on to Trenance Veor and Tere Bean, passing open fields. The Cove Road which ran through Trenance Vean and Garrow was a narrow straight cart track which led up to the Downs in the direction of Teneriffe and Daroose.

At Trenance Veor the Cove Road branched. One lane turned sharp left before the farm buildings and continued over the river, along the "Ghost Hill" road towards Teneriffe and Predannack Wartha. The road continued through the Trenance Veor and Tere Bean farm site before then diverging again. One lane followed the "ridge" towards the site where now lies the Coastguard cottages and Mullion Cove Hotel. This track allowed access to the ancient and complex strip fields or Stitches which covered the hillside while the second ran towards the Cove past the orchards. This part of the "Cove Road" took a route which followed the lower edge of the northern side of the river valley, avoiding "Creggier" or Criggan Mill, down to the Cove before turning back on itself in a sharp hairpin at the foreshore. It then followed the southern edge of the valley back towards Criggan Mill, and then climbing the southern valley side in a zig zag route past the site of one of the Mullion Cliff quarries and up towards Predannack Wartha village, the Soaprock Quarries and the Copper mine.

t) The road which turned south before Trenance Veor is today known as the "Ghost Hill" road. Up the steep hill on the right is the turning for the old Ghostcroft Copper Mine ,and then on towards Teneriffe Farm and the turning for Predannack Wartha near where are located some of the Soapstone Quarries. This was the main 18th and early 19 century mining and quarrying area of Mullion Parish.

u) Local residents insist that the Predannack Wartha village was as important, if not more so than Mullion at that time. Rev. Harvey wrote in 1875 *"As regards the soil the greater part of the Parish rests on a bed of serpentine, and strangers are wont to form large ideas of the vastness of our riches when we tell them that we not only build our houses, but even pave our roads with serpentine."(4)* Some of the serpentine and in fact soapstone from the quarries was used on the roads. A map published in Harvey (1875) which originated in Lakes "Parochial History of the County of Cornwall" indicates the path taken by the roads and the lanes which went over the Downs between farm and hamlets. Daroose, the site of a large quarry, for example, was recorded there as a farm unit called "Dorios". Today, there still exists a track running from there to Predannack Woollas, past Windyridge Farm, south along the footpath over the nearby stream and up across the Downs in the direction of another old isolated farm site called Jollytown.

By 1770, after 20 years of quarrying, the farmers, agricultural workers, quarry workers and fishermen of Mullion would have been part of the same community. Transport by sea was often affected by bad weather and sea conditions but there is some evidence that cargoes were loaded onto boats with shallow draughts and ferried around the coast or out to waiting seagoing vessels. The weather and sea conditions would undoubtedly have had an effect upon both the quarrying and the transport. Although this example is much later, in May 1836 the West Briton reported on a request for a breakwater in Mounts Bay. *"We understand that during the late prevailing winds from N,NE, the Mounts Bay has presented quite an interesting scene being crowded with vessels of various descriptions, windbound, no less than from 250 to 300, riding at anchor in the roads, exclusive of a vast number which took shelter in the piers of Penzance and St. Michaels Mount. We are informed by a correspondent that had the wind shifted suddenly to southward, and blown equally hard,(as sometimes happens) a great portion of this fine fleet of vessels would,in all probability be stranded, whereas with a proposed breakwater they may at all times ride within it in perfect safety in any wind."(25)*

In an East wind, which could often blow for 2 or 3 weeks at a time, the "Mullion Roads" and the west coast of the Lizard would often be full of ships at anchor taking shelter waiting for the wind to change in order that they could navigate past the Lizard and into the English Channel. Later in the 19th Century there was even a call for a breakwater between the mainland near the Vro and Mullion Island for the same reason.

The sea has always been important for the Cornish people. Smuggling or "Free trading" as it was called by those who took part, was an activity which was common in the 18th Century throughout Devon and Cornwall ..... and in fact most of the country. If all stories are taken as true, it was regarded locally as an acceptable day to day activity brought about by a need to bolster a poor existence. Smuggled commodities such as Brandy were one fifth of the English price, while tea was one sixth.

In September 1762, 3 East Indian trading ships from China anchored off Falmouth for 3 weeks and sold china, muslin, silk, arrack (a middle eastern liquor) and cotton goods worth £20,000 to local boats, tax free, unhindered by the Customs.(26) The Revenue men, engaged by the Government to control smuggling around the Coast were not popular, and there was evidence of collusion and avoidance in taking action against the smugglers. The Lizard Coast was no exception.

An official entry by the customs collector in Penzance in June 1775 said the following, *"... the whole coast is principally inhabited by a lot of smugglers under the domination of fishermen, it is next to an impossibility for the officers of the revenue to intercept any of these goods after they are landed, unless by chance a trifling matter. The smugglers escort their goods in large parties when on shore. A few nights ago,... the officers, being on the look-out, saw a boat come ... ashore near where the officers had secreted themselves, and the crew began to land the goods. The officers interfered, and attempted to make a seizure of said boat and goods; but a blunderbuss was immediately presented to one of their breasts, and the smugglers, with great imprecations, threatened their lives. The officers, not being in sufficient force, were glad to get off, and the boat reshipped the goods and went off again. We humbly beg leave to remark the smugglers were never on this coast more rife than at present, nor less goods taken in proportion to the quantity supposed to be smuggled."(27)*

Peter Starling of the Caughley Society investigating Gew Graze

One Revenue man, Captain Pellew, working out of Falmouth at this time, took his Revenue appointment very seriously and with two armed Revenue Cutters, the Hawk with 14 guns and the Lark with 12 guns kept them constantly at sea.

One of the most notorious of smugglers was a man called Thomas Welland, a Dover man who ran an armed lugger called the "Happy-Go-Lucky" with 14 guns on board, and a crew of 30. He and his crew were part of a substantial smuggling fraternity from Cawsand. He had vowed that he would never be taken alive and so it proved. The cutters, (they later came to be known as "Cruisers"), were sent to deal with him, and on the 4th April 1786 Edward Pellew, later Lord Exmouth, who was captaining the "Hawk", along with the "Lark" surprised the "Happy-Go -Lucky" at anchor near Mullion Island, in the shadow of the Mullion Cove Quarries. She was forced to cut her cable and flee west but she was caught and fired upon with "grape and cannister" killing Wellard and the Chief Mate and wounding 12 of the crew, resulting in their surrender. One of the cargoes trafficked by these smugglers were fighting game-cocks and when the Revenue men went on board there were cocks fighting on deck, having had their coops destroyed in the skirmish.(28)

On land, it is likely that many of the workers engaged in the mining of the soaprock

Quarry running inland from Gew Graze beach

Lund Quarries

18th century soapstone working
Gew Graze beach

'Drift' into soapstone at Gew Graze

were also copper miners and may have lived locally. No established dwellings are so far known although there is a suggestion that the property known as Caunce Head at Predannack Wartha, a few hundred yards from Penruddock was the cottage of one of the mine captains. It is known that miners could walk 4 or 5 miles to and from work each day and may have combined alternative employments in the fishing and agriculture industry when the weather was inclement. There is evidence of a small community living above the valley on the Downs above Gew Graze at a location called Jollytown, and he nearest villages were Mullion , St. Keverne ,Ruan Minor and Landwednack. It has been described as neither "Jolly" nor a "Town" but more likely to be cottages close to a farm, now abandoned. It is likely that after the quarrying disappeared these properties may have gone into decline and any stone reused. Jollytown was a small farming community and some local Mullion residents recall their families living there. There is also the Windmill at Kynance of which it is reported that "people would bring their grain for miles to be ground."

The Rev. Harvey writes rather unkindly about "Jolly Town" in his book a hundred years later in 1875, "Mullyon, Its History,Scenery and Antiquities, *"But let us away again over the Downs to Jolly Town- a jovial place indeed!. Can you imagine anything more dreary or desolate? Look every way, can you see even a shrub? Here is an attempt at grass to be sure, but whatever can have induced the first settler to fix on such a spot.? There is positively no road by which to approach the cot, and in winter the down all around you is ankle deep in mud and water. It is a nice airy situation indeed and if you are fond of solitude this is the spot for you, just the place of which you might predicate that it is about 5 miles from anywhere. We might now run down that valley to Gue Greze , and the soap rock, but we will leave that for another day and pass on to Predannack Head."*(29) A local story does exist that there were miners cottages in the area of Jolly Town, but at the moment there is no documentary proof of this.

8. The first soapstone licences

This section of the book intends to present some details of the people who were involved with the earliest attempts to create what was known as steatitic porcelain using soapstone obtained from the Lizard Coast. They include, not only the potters and quarrymen, their mine captains and agents but also the people who owned both the land and the mineral rights on that land. Some only lasted for a few years but they are all remembered by the quality of the porcelain they produced. Many went on to become part of hugely successful manufacturing businesses such as at Worcester while others progressed through mergers and changes in ownership to become household names.

BENJAMIN LUND 1692-1768

The first man to be granted a Licence to quarry for soapstone on the west coast of the Lizard was a Quaker called Benjamin Lund. In the first Soapstone Licence he was described as a Merchant of the City of Bristol. The landowner was John West of Bury St. Edmunds who owned the land at Gew Greaze, part of Erisay Manor in 1748.(30)

Soapstone quarrying was dealt with by an application to the owners of the mineral rights for a lease, known as an Indenture or Licence. The owners of the mineral rights could charge a lease rent of so many guineas per annum and could demand payment of lords dues which was a set payment for every ton of marketable material ranging from10 shillings to 5 pound per ton. There was usually a minimum amount required to be extracted each year, and failure could result in the Lease being revoked. The Licences were official legally binding handwritten contracts which set out the way that the miners were to employ their skills, the equipment they could use, the methods they could adopt and the dates for weighing of the soapstone before shipment and the payment of the rent and any dues. Although Stannary Law only applied to Tin Mining the rules applied to the Soapstone Licences were similar.

The soapstone once quarried varied in quality and had to be hand sorted, packed into casks and weighed before being sent to the potteries. At the potteries it would be crushed at a mill and mixed with pipeclay, seat earth, frit, flint and lime in specific proportions, which in many cases was kept exceptionally secret from competitors. In 1748 Lund visited Cornwall to arrange for the lease of the soaprock deposits described by Borlase. The Lease allowed him *"to draw the soapy rock from Gewcrease in the parish of Mullion,Cornwall"*.(30) See appendix for details of Licence. It was valid for 21 years and with an expiry date in 1770. It would have been required to be renegotiated and renewed if the process was to be continued. Lund had to obtain the labour, organise the opening up of the deposit by quarrymen, employ people to sort the soapstone into separate categories, and the packing of the material into barrels, as well as shipment by sea to Bristol.

In Bristol, preparations were being made to start production with the acquisition of other raw materials which included pipe clay from north Devon, glass frit, potters flint, lime and zaffre (roasted cobalt ore for blue and white colouring). Production of his porcelain started in 1749, the all white "blanc de chine" and the blue on white Nankin ware.

In 1749 he was noted advertising locally in Bristol for apprentices where, *"they shall learn the art of pottery, as practiced in Staffordshire"*. Staffordshire was best known as a producer of Earthenware at that time, and had a ready source of experienced workers. The main wares made by Lund were jugs, sauceboats, tea pots, coffee pots and some figurines, decorated after the Chinese fashion. Despite his evident early success not all went right for Lund as it was during this early phase of setting up the business that the unfortunate Lund also lost his wife Christobel through illness in December 1749.

The Licence allowed the agent, Lund, the following; *"to break up, take and carry away such parts and parcells as he and they shall think proper of all that soft rock commonly called or known by the name of the soapyrock lying in Gewgreaze Cove within the tenement or Great Inclosure called or known by the name of Kinance in the parish of Mullion in the County of Cornwall... and also to dig or search for ye same or ye like clays or rocks in and throughout those parts of the said tenement or inclosure which now or late were in ye tenure or occupation of Barnard Richards Richard Sampson and James and John Harry or any or either of them their or any of their undertenant or undertenants and to raise break up take and carry away ye same to and for his and their own use and uses and at his or their own wills and pleasures (PROVIDED and so as ye said Benjamin Lund.... and all workmen labourers and others to be employed by or under him do as little damage as possible to ye said tenement ..."*

Google view Gew Graze

The first Soapstone Licence issued on the 7th of March 1748 was for a term of 21 years and Lund would be required to pay the lease rent of 10 shillings per ton (50 new pence/ton), or a proportionate amount for less than a ton. The minimum amount to be taken each year was 20 tons (20.32 metric tons). It is not known how this figure was arrived at since no soapstone had previously been quarried and it may have been based on estimates of visible deposits or early tests carried out to remove some soapstone, rather than estimates of requirements by the potter. Perhaps early experiments with the steatite did take place but were not in amounts sufficient to warrant licensed removal.(30)

Pengersick Point

Other than the Licence itself there is little known about the numbers of miners involved or the methods of working the soaprock. The area covered by the Licence was defined according to the overall ownership of the land and the boundaries of the tenements which existed at that time. Landowners changed frequently as did occupation of tenements and in areas of Common Land the practice created some difficulties. The area available to search for soapstone was not exclusive to Gew Graze itself, but prospecting was allowed inland. It would appear that all the soapstone taken from the initial quarries was that which was easily visible on or in the cliffs. The quarries today remain as a series of serpentine "rock islands" just to the north of Gew Graze Beach. They are now worked out , but there are small amounts still visible from inaccessible areas of the cliff. It may have been possible for small boats to lie up off the quarries in calm conditions, but when this was not possible the soapstone would be raised up the side of the cliffs in buckets using winches.

Before any soaprock could be shipped, it had to be sorted and weighed in the presence of the landowner or his agent, and accounts would have to be kept. Some of the later accounts still survive and some destroyed but some probably may still remain in owners archives.

Stemples, referred to in the Licence were a form of wooden steps used in tin and copper mining, usually a wooden bar set between notches in rock walls.

The site is not easily accessible today as indicated by John Penderill-Church, the late researcher and Historian for ECC quarries who wrote the following in a letter to Henry Sandon in 1979 when he took a fact finding trip to the Lizard, *"When I reached Gew Graze, the mist turned to heavy rain, before I could descend safely to get samples or take photographs. I tried to get down but slipped on the wet turf and descended some thirty feet in the most inelegant way, while my dog … ran circles round me thinking it was a new game. … The original quarry is down near the waters edge. The soapstone has been scraped out of a long narrow cleft between unaltered serpentine, until it was scraped clean. Behind this is the Turner-Gallimore cleft and behind this the Flight and Dilwyn cleft. The soapstone occurs where acid magmatic vapours have forced their way along faults and joints in the serpentine, and have converted the parent rocks in the contact zones into steatites (cordierite steatite). The soapstone normally occurs in narrow veins and seams, many of them so narrow that normal quarrying methods would be impractical. The softness of the rock, however enabled it to be extracted successfully by a combination of digging and scraping. On the sloping sides of Gew Graze there are still some narrow veins of soapstone yet unworked , because of the precipitous nature of their location. The name Gew Graze comes from the cornish Gyew Gres-Vein in the middle- which is just what it was – a vein of soft rock in the middle of hard rock."* (31)

Pengersick Quay

His interpretation of the quarry sites cannot be fully verified but there are certainly small deposits of soapstone remaining all along this northern edge of the Cove right up to Pengersick Point and in the direction of Vellan Head. Many people who walk this coast both today and in the past will have experienced the weather conditions he described.

After Lund, other Potteries obtained Licences to quarry along the cliffs to the north west of the Cove, and also inland from the beach along the valley, and to the north east of the cliffs behind the Lund Quarries. The valley is approximately 600 yards in length and some of the worked out remains of these quarries are still visible.

It has been considered that some of the early quarries may have been in the valley itself but descriptions written at the time do not support this view. The beach quarries are only accessible on foot at really low tides, and with great care, but they are accessible in quieter weather from a shallow draught boat. There has long been speculation about how the soapstone was removed from the early quarries. There are reports of people with engravings or prints which show sailing boats close in to soapy cove but these have not yet been verified. Recent observational research in relation to Gew Graze has provided some answers to this question in the form of the newly discovered quay, and will be looked at shortly. It is likely that some was moved along existing lanes or roads to small quays or ports around the coast, but it was eventually transported via the larger coastal routes such as Hayle to Bristol in the same way that Copper and Tin was transported. Many roads and tracks in the 18th century were suitable for little more than the movement of livestock, horse drawn carts or pack horses. It should also be noted that there were no large communities close to Gew Graze with Landwednack (Lizard), Ruan Minor and Mullion being over 2 miles away in a straight line … longer and more arduous on foot or existing rural lanes.

Rock cut landing stage
Pegersick Quay

A first hand account exists of a visit to Gew Graze, and also Lunds Pottery at Bristol in 1750, made by Dr Richard Pococke, then Bishop of Meath, who travelled throughout Britain.

Iron mounting point Pegersick Quay

On October 13th 1750 he wrote; "*We went nine miles to the South near as far as the Lizard Point, to see the Soapy Rock, which is a little opening in the cliff, where a rivulet runs over a vein of Soapy-rock into the sea, the lode or vein running along the bottom of the valley: it is about four feet wide, most of it mixed with red, like terra lemnia, and the stone or walls on each side are of the same colour, and they find some of it hard and unfit for use even in the vein; there are white patches of it, which is mostly valued for making porcelain, and they get five pounds a ton for it, for the manufacture of porcelain, now carrying on at Bristol, there being much trouble in separating the white from the red; but they have received instructions lately not to be so exact in separating it, probably on their not being able to afford it at that price. There is a narrow vein of green earth near it, and about twenty yards west a small vein of white, which seems to me not to be so soapy a nature. It feels like soap, and being so dear it must be much better that pipe clay; there is a vein of something of the like nature at the Lizard Point.*"(32)

Remains of drill hole

On November 2nd 1750 he wrote again to his mother : "*I went to see a manufacture lately established here, by one one of the principal manufacturers at Limehouse which failed. It is at a glasshouse, and is called Lound's China house. They have two sorts of ware, one called stone china, which has a yellow cast, both in the ware and in the glazing, that I suppose is made of pipe clay and calcined flint. The other they call old china; this is whiter, and I suppose this is made of calcined flint and the soapy rock at Lizard Point which is 'tis known they use. This is painted blue and some is white, like the old china of a yellowish cast; another kind is white with a bluish cast, and both are called fine ornamental white china. They make very beautiful white sauce boats, adorned with reliefs of festoons, which sell for sixteen shillings a pair*".(32)

PENGERSICK QUAY

Many academics and historians have walked the Soaprock Coast including the area known as Gew Graze but there is still information waiting to be discovered on the ground.

In 1958 the late Dr Bernard Watney, a former chairman of the English Ceramic Circle (ECC) wrote, "*At Gew Graze the little rivulet still runs down to the sea but it is now difficult to find any soapy rock against the granite* [actually, serpentine] *boulders. Some say that there was once a small jetty in the cove for the shipment of soaprock but most of it was probably taken overland to the Port of Hayle*" Back in 1958, a jetty was never located.(33)

Pure white Soapstone - Pengersick

In May 2011 I was visited by Peter Starling who is an active and enthusiastic member of the Caughley Porcelain Society who has an interest in Soapstone. We visited Gew Graze and viewed the remains of the early quarries, along with the sites at Mullion Cove and on the walk we were able to collect some pieces of soapstone for Peter to use in his talks to the Caughley Society. On our return we visited a local village shop in Mullion when a chance remark in a conversation with Mike, the owner, brought mention of the existence of old iron mooring rings at a site known as 'Old Mullion'. This was confirmed by local fishermen and a site was identified for consideration near to Pengersick Point.

One of the unanswered questions relating to the quarries was how, and from where, at Gew Graze the many tons of soapstone were transported. Pengersick Point is at the northern side of Gew Graze Cove, north west of the known 18th century soapstone cliff quarries. It is about 600 yards from the site of the first Lund quarries.

About 100 yards east of the Point is a sheltered narrow rectangular inlet, looking out towards Pigeon Ogo (Pigeon Hugo) which is across the bay on the south side of Gew Graze. The inlet is approximately 50 yards from open water. The external width of the inlet is approximately 18-20 yards and narrows slightly inwards to about 10-12 yards near the base of the cliff.

The entrance to the inlet runs steeply down from the flat Predannack Downs and has a high serpentine cliff face to the east and lower serpentine cliffs to the west which in turn run north towards Vellan Head.

It is one of the very few areas along this section of cliff which allows someone to physically walk from the top of the cliff to the sea at the bottom.

A close inspection of the site has revealed the following information. At sea level, to the west side of the inlet is a low rocky promontory. The rock adjacent to the inlet shows evidence of having being cut into the bedrock and shaped to form a quay or wharf, by the creation of a horizontal platform about 10 foot in width with a vertical backwall. Erosion of the serpentine cliffs is a continuous process and in the landward end of the bottom of the inlet today lie some large boulders of serpentine which have recently fallen from the cliffs on the eastern side, reducing the open length of the inlet by several yards. The platform sits just above the high water mark. At low water mark there is at least 10-15 foot of water still available, and most importantly shelter from the winds especially from north, north west, west and east.

On or near the backwall of the rock platform there are the remains of at least 12 vertical holes, still visible in half profile, bored into the rock. The rock appears to have been hewn out to form the quay. The rock would have been drilled with hand tools. The longest hole is about 2 foot in length and approximately 1 inch in diameter. (A fifty pence coin can fit into the bottom of the holes) At the bottom of one of the bored holes are iron remains broken off at ground level which may be the remains of a metal boring tool broken off in the hole just below the surface. Examination of the remains show that it is triangular in shape. As a result of enquiries with local mine museums it seems that this may be a rare find. There are tools of this type known from the 18th century of which the first 8 or 9 inches are triangular and the rest hexagonal or round. In mining terms these hand tools were used by two or more men. One man held the tool while the other hit it into the hole with a large hammer. In some cases in mine

Quarry trench example 1

Quarry trench example 2

Quarry trench example 3

workings two men would alternatively hit the boring tool with hammers in unison to increase the speed of boring. The tool would turned by hand as the hole deepened. In this case a number of holes are visible which would indicate that the section of rock was either blown out with powder charges or chiselled out using other metal tools and possibly wedges. There are other holes with tight fitting metal remains which may be the remnants of iron mountings.

There are two large flat bottomed rock cut niches above the quay area, and in one vertical backwall the remains of two substantial rusted iron mountings, one of which has a distinctive protruding profile. On the upper surface of the promontory there is also an iron mounting still with the metal "eye" which would have contained a mooring ring, rusted but still in good condition and situated on a flat rock above the quay.

There is evidence of a "foot worn" walkway about 8-10 foot wide cut into the bedrock for part of the route down to the quay from the Downs forming what could be described as the loading/unloading area. The evidence points to this being the site of an old sheltered quay or wharf, created, or adapted and used in its current form by the men who quarried for soapstone. Despite being some distance from any large areas of habitation it shows evidence of being in use as sheltered mooring for a long period of time. The soapstone would have been brought to the quay over the Downs by horse and cart from the quarries where a windlass or other device would be used to transfer it down the slope to the quayside where it would be loaded into small sailing boats. In order to do this it is likely that there would have been lifting gear and tackle constructed on the site to load the soapstone into the boats.

This may have been similar to operations conducted at quarries such as at Tintagel on the north west cornish coast. Whether the soapstone was graded and weighed before being transported to the quay on this site is unknown, but if not it would probably have been taken to a local sorting area, possibly at Mullion where these operations could be conducted, and then weighed and reshipped to a port such as Hayle.

There appears to be a strong similarity between this site and that of Tintagel where slate was similarly quarried. William Borlase wrote about a number of stone quarries in Cornwall in his book "The Natural History of Cornwall" published in 1758. In reference to a stone quarry in North Cornwall, away from the sea he wrote on the use of tools, *"...the masses are first raised rough from the rock by wedges driven by sledges of iron and contain ... superficial squares of stone, as soon as this mass is freed by one man, another stone cutter, with a strong wide chizel and mallett, is ready to cleave it to its proper thickness.... all the flat (slate) is carried with no small danger, from the plot where it rises, on mens backs, which are guarded from the weight by a leather apron or rather cushion... and then horses are ready to take them off, and then carry them by tale to the person that buys them"*.(34)

Of transport from a quarry near Tintagel he wrote, *"If this quarry was situated near to a good harbour, much greater advantage might be made of it; but all the stone exported must be carried by land to a little Cove called Portissick (Port Isaac) four miles off on the North coast, where no ships of burden can safely take in their loading; and what is not*

Merthen Quay

Merthen Quay

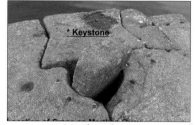
Merthen Quay

exported is dispersed in the neighbourhood by an expensive land carriage".(34)

Research from the Tintagel slate quarries such as Lanterdean, Gull Point, Dria and Bagalow, provides a guide as to how the quarries would have operated on the coast. Some of those quarries were believed to have been worked as early as the 1400s, with the last closing in 1937. At Tintagel today slate waste lies on the cliff side down to the sea. Back in the 18th Century there would have been a number of quarries in operation. At that time a boat would be moored below the cliffs, and a derrick perched on the cliff edge, which would be used to load the slate. A wharf was also constructed at Penhallic Point where the cliff edge was cut back to form a 100 foot vertical cliff face. Ships would lie against this cliff in the natural deep water berth, and the slate would be lowered by crane. Strong points would be built into the cliff face and cradles and buckets could be let down the cliff face to enable removal of slate.

At Gull Point Quarry there is a platform where a blindfolded donkey would walk in a circle to activate the winding gear. This was not an unusual feature of life in the 18th Century for it was a system also used in agriculture by farmers. Along the Tintagel coast you can still find the ruins of splitting sheds and anchor blocks for the donkey powered winches. The winches were used to wind up the slate blocks for splitting and the narrow paths you find there today are often old donkey tracks.(35)

Boats would often find it difficult to lie up under the Gew Graze cliffs and it is suggested that the miners operated a similar system to remove the soapstone from the cliffs here and at Mullion, with the soapstone cleaned or spalled, sorted and weighed before being transported. The use of Pengersick Point as a quay is confirmed by the fact that well over a hundred years ago a local Predannack Farmer called Shepherd used the site for his fishing boat and would walk from Predannack to and from the quay to where the boat was docked.

A NEW SOAPSTONE QUARRY

Near to the top of the site there is a ridge running north to south. This ridge overlooks the cliffs to the west which lie between Pengersick Point and Vellan Head. This site directly overlooks the sea.

At the top of the ridge there is a row of large rocks which appear to have been placed there by hand. These rocks overlook a gulley which is visible running down the side of the cliff. It can be seen that this is in fact the opening to a trench about 4-6 foot wide and about 5 foot deep containing large angular boulders of serpentine. The base of the trench appears to have been worked, and at the sides and base of this trench are exposed veins of off-white or pale green soapstone. The trench continues about 15 yards (13m) west down to the edge of the cliff before curving to the north along the cliff edge. There are at least 2 other similar trenches which run parallel to the first, down the side of the cliff for about 15 yards and they then join the main trench at the lower end. There is evidence of soapstone veins along the whole length of these gullies, both pale green in colour and some pure white. Examination on the ground shows that there is evidence of soapstone up to 6 inches in thickness along almost the whole length of the trench and it is evident that this is a Quarry Trench dug to remove soapstone. The quarry trench expands to be about 10yards (9m) in width before narrowing and then running north for the whole length of the cliff up to Vellan Head, where excavation work appears to stop.

There is no obvious Soapstone Licence within the public domain covering this section of the cliff making it difficult to date, but several tons of soapstone would have been removed from this site. It lies to the north of Gew Graze and may have formed a quarry recorded as being on the Predannack Downs.

There is also some evidence that right around the base of the cliff on Pengersick Point itself a trench has also been cut which has now been been weathered by the sea, leaving a south facing semi circular pool visible at low tide.

There seems little doubt that the soapstone would have been removed over the ridge, down the slope and taken by boat from the Pengersick Jetty, only some 80 yards away, and the evidence points to widespread quarrying activity.

The existence of this quay and the newly described soapstone quarry has been brought to the attention of the County Archaeologist and it may be possible to further investigate the site of Gew Graze in the future. At this stage it has not been possible to identify which factory had the licence for this venture but it does further indicate that there is much to be learnt about the soapstone working in the area and hopefully it will be possible to encourage a further investigation into this fascinating under researched period of Cornish History.

The First Worcester Factory at Warmstry House. Engraving from the Gentlemans Magazine 1752 (37)

TRANSPORT BY LAND-MERTHEN QUAY

There now exists some firm evidence of transport of soapstone by sea but there is recorded evidence of transport by land in the early 1760s in the form of records of shipments from Merthen Quay which lies on the North side of the Helford Estuary , nine miles from Mullion. Charleston and Mallet were able to locate an account book from the 1770's showing various harbour dues paid to the Manor of Merthen.(36)

The entries were as follows;
1761, April 24th *"For ditto (Killage and Anchorage) of Cap. Westcotes Sloop for Sopeyrock*   *8d*
1762, August 6th *"To ditto" of Cap. Westcotts sloop for Sopeyrock*   *8d*
1764, June 4th *"Killage and Anchorage of Capt Tho Johns sloop for soperock"*   *8d*
1765, December 6th *"To ditto" of Cap. Wecouts sloop for Soppey rock"*   *8d*

The existence of these records provides invaluable information about the movement of the soaprock by sea using a sloop. Sloops, for their size, around 50 feet long and 18 feet in breadth were described as being "a jack of all trades", being fast agile and with a shallow draught. Due to their agility they were also often used by pirates and smugglers, which led to the Navy and Revenue Officers also adopting their use, along with the heavier cutters as armed patrol vessels. What it also shows is that the soapstone was moved through here for many years, at all times of the year, despite quarrying taking place mainly in the summer months.

I have had the opportunity through permission of the quay owners and the Vyvyan family of Merthen Manor to visit the privately owned site of Merthen Quay. Merthen Manor in the 16th Century was owned by the Reskymer family. It was sold to the Vyvyans in 1629 in whose ownership it has remained. It is situated on the northern side of the Helford estuary on high ground leading down to the busy Helford Creek. The Helford Estuary at that time was busy. Gweek had been the port for Helston since the 13th Century and as there were a number of quays along the Helford they were in use for transporting among other things granite and mineral ores from the Constantine area as well as bringing in, for example limestone, coal and timber.

MERTHEN QUAY

The Quay is of Historical interest and dates back several hundred years. It is approached by an ancient wooded track approximately 6 foot wide cut into bedrock and with a central gulley which drained water into the Helford. (It has also been suggested that the central gulley helped keep a horse and a heavily laden cart on a straight line down the narrow track) Within 30 yards of the quayside lie the well preserved remains of what is believed to be a lime kiln which still contains the circular kiln with its lining of burnt bricks still bearing the yellow glassy remnants of past use.

The quayside is composed of large locally sourced rectangular granite blocks accurately set together on a base of upright slate sheets which in turn lie on the bedrock of the river. It is approximately 50 foot (15.2m) in length. In the centre of the quay is a star shaped stone adjacent to an aperture which would have housed the mechanism or "crane" for loading and unloading boats.

It is to such an area that in the 1760s the soaprock was transported by cart from Mullion, through Gweek and on to Merthen, to the quayside and off to Bristol, Worcester or Liverpool to be crushed and used to make porcelain.

In the 1750s, being on the eastern side of the Lizard it may have been a site used to transport to Vauxhall in London. Because of its tidal advantages and sheltered location Merthen was still in use as an active quay until at least the 1920s.

There were a number of types of boats in use at this time and their use in coastal mining was not unknown. In 1778 Tin was found in the coastal rocks at Wherrytown at the eastern end of Penzance Promenade. The tin-bearing rocks were only exposed at low tide which created a problem for the miners. A stone collar with a wooden tower on top had to be built around the top of the shaft which at high tide was 20 foot (6m) below sea level. The mine had to be emptied each day before the ore was removed and it was either taken away in flat bottomed shallow draught boats called Wherries or simply carried away at low tide. The soaprock Mine Captains would have had a very similar problem to overcome no more than a few miles away on the opposite side of Mounts Bay at Gew Graze and Mullion Cove on the Lizard. The use of small shallow water boats to carry cargo out to waiting ships was known on the Lizard right up to the end of the 19th Century.(36a)

9. Dr. John Wall,
Soaprock and the Lund connection to Worcester

Dr John Wall, was born near Worcester in 1708, became a qualified Medical Doctor, a Fellow of Merton College, and a Bachelor of Physic at St Thomas` Hospital in London. In 1750 he and an apothecary William Davis had experimented with a new method of making porcelain in Davis`shop in Broad Street Worcester. One of their aims was to try and produce a successful hard paste and durable porcelain able to withstand boiling water, at a time when tea drinking was becoming more and more popular and there was an obvious need for new commercial products. At the time of this venture the town of Worcester was beginning to experience a decline in its main businesses of manufacturing gloves and the weaving of woollen broadcloth and was in need of regeneration. Porcelain making was an untried industry with many new potteries failing at an early stage and it was perhaps, seen as a speculative entry into a new market. Most importantly it did possess all the requirements of the new business in access to raw materials through local ports, access to fuel for the kilns, a ready supply of labour, including trained labour, a ready market for the product, advertising facilities, and a growing distribution network. And, of course, financial backing.

Wall and Davis persuaded a group of 13 other local businessmen to back their discovery with investment in new premises at Warmstry House at Worcester. The premises, which they converted, was an old mansion house near to the Cathedral, with a garden fronting onto the River Severn.

A lease was taken out on 16th May 1751 and on the 4th June the fifteen partners signed a deed to officially establish the Worcester Tonquin Manufacture, and a 21 year lease was agreed.

The principle shareholder William Bayliss, a physician, invested £675, Edward Cave owner of the "Gentlemans Magazine", from

London invested £562 10s, as did Richard Holdship, a glover from Worcester. Richard Holdship, along with Robert Hancock were experienced engravers who went on to work with the transfer printing technique used by Worcester from 1757. Josiah Holdship, Richards brother, a maltster invested £450, John Thorneloe £337 10s and the remaining partners including Wall invested £225. Other investors included Samuel Bradley, a silversmith who supervised the making of the moulds. There were two experienced potters, John Lyes and Robert Podmore, and to preserve the secrecy of the formula for the porcelain they were given extra payments to *"secure their fidelity."*…. but this later backfired when Podmore left, taking the porcelain formula with him. The total capital behind the partnership was £4500. Word of Benjamin Lunds success in Bristol had reached the ears of the Worcester directors and they made an approach to him. It is not known whether the Worcester interest came about as a result of Lunds apparent success with the porcelain production or whether it was because of the apparent competition but Richard Holdship, like Lund a Quaker, started negotiations at the end of 1751. Early in 1752 a price of £1700 was agreed to purchase the Bristol company. Lund had to agree not to divulge the secrets of his process to anyone except the Worcester partners. As there was only £300 left in the Worcester concern at this time, Richard Holdship agreed to purchase on behalf of his partners, coming to an arrangement that he would hold the soaprock licence, selling the soaprock to his partners at £18/ton.(37)

Dr. John Wall

On 1st February 1752 the Lund factory in Bristol was taken over by Richard Holdship at Worcester and the formula and the expertise of the workers were transferred up the River Severn to Worcester. Most importantly for Worcester was that the Soapstone Licence taken out by Lund was also transferred with the deeds and proved invaluable to their business. With the money Lund was able to pay off his debts, but he was now 60 years of age. He was obliged to keep the soapstone recipe secret and under the agreement with Worcester could make no more porcelain. Lund and his foreman Thomas Franks (who eventually went to work for William Cookworthy) were taken on by Worcester as modellers and mould makers and remained there until 1757or1758 before retiring to Bristol. Whilst there Lund got to know William Cookworthy and took a keen interest in his projects.

Early Worcester porcelain

Lund died on New Years Day 1768 at the age of 75. He was buried in the "Friends Burial Ground" at Fryars, Bristol.(19a)

Shortly after the completion of the Lund takeover an article appeared in the Gentlemans Magazine of 1752, owned by Edward Cave, stated that *"The sale of this manufacture will begin at the Worcester Music Meeting on September 20th ,with great variety of ware, and tis said, at a moderate price."* This form of marketing of the Worcester porcelain was a normal procedure among potteries and other industries in the 18th century and used to advertise their products. The early wares included teawares, pots, sauceboats and pickle dishes, along with some vases. The early decoration was in blue and white and copied the chinese form. It had a huge advantage over other pottery products at this time in that it did not crack or break in hot water. The production process was kept exceptionally secret and the location of the business on the river was critical due to the transport requirements of materials. At the premises there was a

View of the Worcester Factory and the River by Paul Sandby (Worcester Porcelain Museum) 1778

secret room on the ground floor where the porcelain bodies were made. Robert Podmore and John Lyes of the original directors were evidently privy to the secret. Coal was used in the process with 10-12 tons of fuel required to fire one ton of finished wares as the wares had to be fired seven or eight times before completion. However, even though the public had access to the pottery, there was the room within the building where no one was allowed to visit, and this held the secret of the formula for the porcelain mix.

The Soaprock was probably shipped from a number of locations in Cornwall. It is known that early loads were shipped in casks from Hayle, on the West of England run to Bristol where they would be unloaded and placed in barges to be transported to Worcester, probably via Gloucester. The barges were pulled up the River Severn by hand. From January 1st 1763 a 9 year lease was taken out for the soaprock to be processed elsewhere. A grinding mill at Astley Forge Mill was added to the manufactory situated at Glasshampton Brook, in the Parish of Astley some 12 miles upsteam from Worcester. The crushed soaprock was then returned to Worcester for use in the production of the porcelain.(38)

Astley Forge Mill has recently been successfully excavated by the North Worcester Archaeology Group.(36b)

Richard Holdships financial involvement eventually led him to be made a bankrupt in 1760 having over extended his finances in the partnership deal. He had taken out the lease on the Warmstry House site only 19 days before the partnership deeds were signed, purchasing the Lease of a soaprock quarry and putting up extensive new buildings on the Warmstry House site (37) The transfer of the soaprock licence to Worcester had allowed them to continue quarrying at Gew Graze. It is worth noting that ownership of Erisay Manor passed from West to Edward Boscawen, Lord Falmouth in 1757 and Worcester took out a new lease on Gew Graze from him.

By 1753 aristocrats and members of the landed gentry, including the Marquis of Rockingham were buying pint and half pint mugs, cups with handles, chocolate cups and saucers and milk pots made from Worcester Porcelain. By 1754 Porcelain was being sold to the Trade through a warehouse in London and also through Samuel Bradleys shop in Worcester. Edward Cave, one of the directors, died in 1754 and a second partnership was introduced which brought in 9 new directors. These included Rev Benjamin Blayney, Robert Blayney, Rev. David and Mary Henry, and Thomas Vernon MP. By 1754 a Sale took place at the Royal Exchange Coffee house in London which advertised an auction of *"About 40,000 pieces of China Ware of the Worcester Manufactory"*. There was no description of the Wares except that *"The commodity will speak for itself"*.(37)

By 1755 Worcester was making the some of the best English blue and white porcelain tea wares available as well as expensive coloured sets and had a large warehouse in the capital at London House, Aldersgate. Items were often sold by the dozen with good discounts given for prompt payment.(37)

In 1755, The Prince George sailed from Canton with a cargo which included 80,000

Advert for the sale of Worcester Porcelain Company after the expiry of the first 21year lease.

pieces of chinese porcelain, most of which was blue and white. This included over 10,000 individual plates. A further 6 ships owned by the East India Company sailed from Canton in 1755 all carrying porcelain amongst their cargo.

There was now competition. In 1756 sales of blue and white porcelain were taking place at the Castle Green warehouse in Bristol and advertisements were appearing in such places as Birmingham and the highly fashionable Bath. Knowledge of how to make porcelain was a closely guarded secret and even today exact details are not released lightly. Unfortunately not everything could rival the Chinese market at this time. Plates, for example, could not be produced without there being firing blemishes and Worcester hardly produced any until this was resolved. In the market place, however, Worcester Teapots with their heat resistance faired better than their rivals which included Chelsea, Bow, Derby and Longton Hall.

By the 1760s Large scale auctions took place on a regular basis highlighting the volume of production and the popularity of the items.

Caerthillian Cliff Quarry

A description by Valentine Green of a factory tour published in 1764 records that the factory was situated in Mardyke, near the River Severn, having it on the west, Warmstry slip on the north, St Albans Church and Fish Street on the east, and the Bishops Palace and the Cathedral on the south. And *"… Upon entrance to it you are conducted into the Counting House on the right hand of the passage, and from thence into the throwing room, where the ware is first formed from the clay. From this you are taken through a narrow passage to the Stove, which, a fire being placed in the centre, equally diffuses its heat to the whole, the ware is placed here to dry gradually thereby preparing it for the succeeding operation. The next room shown is the great hall where the ware is turned upon the lathe. In a little room adjoining, another method it carried on, called, pressing the ware on the wheel.... In a great parlour … is also turning on the lathe, with that part of the business called handling and spouting, hands to cups and spouts to tea pots.... to another pressing room... the clay is pressed only by the hands in the mould. From hence you are conducted to the lower regions of this work, where are …the biscuit kilns in which the ware is first burnt. After passing another stove you enter the dipping or glazing room, in which the ware receives its glaze. From thence to another set of kilns where the glaze ware is burnt. Then crossing the coal yard you are shown a third set called streightening kilns; in an adjoining room, the cases or saggers in which they burn the ware, are made. To the scraping room next shown where the biscuit ware …. is sorted. In the slip house, the different parts of the composition, being first levigated are sifted through fine sieves … blended and dried . In a room adjoining the slip house you are shown a large iron rowl, upwards of 2 tons weight, by the assistance of horses, revolving in a groove, not much unlike a cyder mill. This rowl reduces all the hard bodies made use of in the composition to a fine powder, fit for levigation. You at length enter the painting room, where the ware receives the ornamental part of the process, after burning and assorting is completed for sale."(38a)*

Soapstone vein Caerthillian

'Soft' soapstone Pentreath

Note; To "levigate" is to reduce to a fine powder fit for paste and was the site where the soaprock was initially crushed before the process moved to Astley Forge Mill. However, even though the public had access to the pottery, there was the room within the building where no one was allowed to visit, and this held the secret of the formula for the porcelain mix.

Valentine Green in the same book, quoting from what he described as an anonymous writer in a local newspaper of the time about the Worcester porcelain, " *The body of this last* (the worcester porcelain) *far exceeds all the rest in fineness and whiteness, in which it almost, if not altogether, equals even the finest porcelain of China itself, and is found to be more harder and more durable than the body of any other porcelain whatever. The glazing of it never nips, breaks off or even parts from the body, except by extreme violence and it then discovers no brownness such as is often seen in the ordinary chinese, and almost always after wear in the other kinds of porcelain. It is perfectly clear and transparent . and the finer sort which is enamelled so nearly resembles the ... finest oriental pieces ... that where it has been made in imitation of these, as has often been the case, in order to match and make up setts that have been broken, the difference is scarcely discernible even to judges themselves, and sometimes the Worcester has been mistaken for the foreign. The most valuable part of all ... is the extraordinary strength and cheapness of the common sort of blue and white Worcester porcelain*".(38a)

Rock cut platform Caerthillian

Google Earth view of
Caerthillian and Pentreath

In 1763 they were able to advertise in the Oxford Journal that *"Services of Chinese Porcelain can be made up with Worcester Porcelain so that the difference cannot be discovered"*. In other words they could repair or replace broken or damaged Chinese pieces to an extremely high standard. In 1769 a sale took place in London over several days which included *"An elegant table service, containing 16 oblong dishes, five sizes, a tureen, cover and dish, five dozen table plates, and one dozen soup, all of the marazine-blue enamelled in flowers"* which sold for £21 10s 6d. It is worth pointing out that the early records and account books of the first Worcester factory are unfortunately lost. This is not unusual for early potteries but it would have provided a lot of information about the day to day activities of the company, including their use of soapstone.(38a)

The experience and confidence of the Worcester manufacturers was shown when they went into open competition with the British East India Company which was importing so much porcelain from China. As an example of the quantity of items produced by Worcester between 1771 and 1774 the highly regarded China and enamel painter and decorator James Giles purchased 40-50,000 undecorated pieces of Worcester porcelain for decorating at his London factory in Trafalgar Square. His clients included the daughter of King George the second, the Duke of Marlborough, Duke of Richmond, Duke of Bolton, the Earl of Carlisle, and Sir Egerton Leigh of South Carolina.(37)

On the expiry of the initial 21 year lease the company was put up for sale in January 1772. The advert included reference to buildings and all stock plus *"... the companys interest in the lease of a mine of clay in Cornwall"* The auction sale took place at the Hop Pole Inn in Worcester, and the company was subsequently reconstituted with new partners; Dr Wall, William Davis Senior and Junior, Robert Hancock, Thomas Vernon and Richard Cook with some changes in the ensuing few years up to 1776.(37)

10. The rise of the porcelain manufacturers

NICHOLAS CRISP AND JOHN SANDERS

Even before the merger between Benjamin Lund and Worcester was in progress other pottery factories were in the process of obtaining a Licence to mine Soaprock. In 1751 Nicholas Crisp, previously a haberdasher and jeweller, entered into partnership with John Sanders, a jeweller and potter at Lambeth, London where they set up the Vauxhall factory producing a soft paste porcelain using soaprock. The factory did not mark its porcelain and little was known about it until a discovery was made that it had erroneously been attributed to Liverpool factory of potter William Ball. The Vauxhall factory was one of a number of once famous but now defunct porcelain factories lining the Thames during the Georgian era including Chelsea (1744-1782), Bow at Stratford. (1747-1776) and Limehouse in the Docklands area (1745-1748) which was only identified in the late 1980s. The factory was described as a three storey premises with trap doors to lower and raise packages between the floors, with a yard and great gates. Bradshaw (1992) and Toppin (1933).(39)

An advertisement in the Public Advertiser in May 1753 described as *"the sale to the public of Vauxhall Porcelain"*. *"Notice of porcelain ware by Mr Sanders. To the Public Near the plate glasshouse Vauxhall, is now to be sold, a strong and useful manufacture of Porcelaine Ware, made there of English Materials"*. The advertisement goes on to describe how up until then, the materials for pottery were sent abroad to Holland , made into delftware and then sold back in England, but now the quality of english earthenware had improved so much that it could equal or better the Dutch ware. However it goes on to describe how the earthenware cannot withstand heat and moisture causing the glaze to crack and break off. It described the qualities of the imported China-ware, *"smooth and as easily cleaned as glass, and at the same time bears the hottest liquors without danger of breaking"* and how the ware produced at Vauxhall was beginning to match these qualities, so *"doing a considerable service to the Publick"*. They obtained permission to mine on the Lizard at a location called Caerthillian Crofts. This included the areas known as Caerthillian (Gothillian Mill), Pentreath and Kynance in the Parish of Landwednack.

On the 24th June 1751 a 10 year soaprock licence was granted to *"Nicholas Crisp in London, a Jeweller, and John Sanders of Lambeth in the County of Surrey, Potter by the Right Honorable Hugh Viscount Falmouth on the Lizard Peninsula, to work upon certain veins or lodes of Mineral Earth commonly called the Soapyrock on that part of Lord Falmouths lands in the parish of Landewednack from the extent of the cliffs next the sea as far east on the course of the said veins as 50 fathoms provided the said 50 fathoms do not extend within one fathom of the several or enclosed lands there and in extent from Gothillian Mill North as far as Chynance within the said Parish of Landewednack as the same is now portioned out and allotted excepting all Tin, Tin Toll works, Copper Ore, Copper works, Lead ore and all other mines minerals and metals. Dues, one guinea per ton."* (30)

Quarrying was only allowed inland to the boundary of enclosed or agricultural land, which appears to be why the Licence restricted the work to 50 fathoms, 300 foot (91m) from the cliffs One application of this limitation can be seen when walking the coastal path. The boundary of enclosed land can be seen today and the walls run but a few feet from the top of the cliff above Caerthillian and Pentreath. The cliffs themselves are unstable and deeply weathered consisting of decomposed serpentine

CAERTHILLIAN CROFTS & PENTREATH

On 24th June 1751 Mary Vere Hunt, landowner at Lanhydrock, granted a 10 year Licence to Crisp and Sanders for *"lands lying or being the commons of Lizzard within the Parish of Landwednack ...."* This Licence, as pointed out in an article written and researched by Sonia Parkinson, mirrors the Licence issued by Lord Falmouth and appears to show that authority to mine the soaprock at this location required multiple permissions from a number of Landowners, sometimes known as the "Lords of the Lizard". This seems to revolve around the frequency of land owners changing in a short period of time and some lands being sold between the Lords without firm boundaries. Permission in the form of a Licence would be required from all landowners in order search and work minerals. Her research showed the existence of papers at a company of Lawyers in London, one set of which was entitled *"Ye account of ye soapy rock sent Lord Falmouth"*, dated 20 Jan 1752. This was believed to refer to soaprock weighed between 13th-15th January 1752. The weight was 31tons 1cwt and 2 quarters at a guinea a ton giving a total due of £32-12s-6d A list with four landowners names, the value in the parish of their holdings in shillings and pence and the pro rata share to which each was entitled, to the nearest farthing was recorded.(30)(30a)

Parish Value of the estates. *(pounds, shillings, pence and farthings)*

Lord Falmouths 5-1-1/2 Share of the above sum	£8	5s 9d 3f
Mrs Hunts (Lanhydrock) 3-0	£4	17s 0d 3f
Mr Robinsons (Bochym) 5-3	£8	9s 10d 1f
Mr Hills 6-9-1/2	£10	19s 8d 3f
TOTAL	£32	12s 5d 2f (30)(30a)

In support of the argument is quoted a record of an entry in the Lanhydrock agent, Francis Coles Record Book of Lanhydrock, dated 7th April 1752 *"By cash from John Pascoe, Lord Falmouths Steward, for your part of the clay dug out of the soap rock at Lizard and weighed off the 14th and 15th days of January last.......... £4-14s-8d"*

The accounts must have been accurately kept by the potters, their mine captains and the agents of the landowners to avoid confusion and comply with the legal requirements of the Licence. Is there a significance in the letter from Gavregan Teppit to Richard Chaffers written on 2nd October 1756 when he says *"he will send about 10 tuns of clay, but was afraid of a disturbance between the Lords of the Land when he weighed it off"*?(40) Dues payable were 1 guinea per ton, but otherwise the Licence appears to continue the pattern of the Lord Falmouth Licence.

MULLION CLIFFS

On 28th February 1752 Mary Hunt the owner of Lanhydrock granted a further Licence to Crisp and Sanders to mine for soaprock *" ..... in the lands of the said Mary Hunt situate and lying and being in the Little Commons or Downs commonly called Goon Vean belonging to and part of the Tenements of Predannack Wartha in the Parish of Mullion in the said county of Cornwall to work the said veins or lodes from the extent of the cliff next the Sea as far East on the course of the said veins or loads as 200 fathoms and in extent from a rock called Porth Pyg north as far as Pedenankea on the South."*

According to the Soaprock Licence, from 28th February 1752, the area known as Mullion Cliffs was quarried for Soaprock. This is part of Mullion Cove itself now, an area of outstanding natural beauty today and visited by thousands of people each year. Inland from the Cove the area consists of steeply sloping land with gorse and scrub vegetation, with rocky Cairns and an occasional enclosed field. The land enclosure process was increasing in the 18th century with tenants clearing land, constructing hedges or walls and cultivating the ground for pasture or grain. The miners were licensed to work up to 200 fathoms 400 yards inland, which would have taken them close to the boundary of the land which included the copper mine of Wheal Providence. Pedenankea or Pedn-Y-Ke , the northern extent of the Licence is situated on the Southern boundary of Pollurian Cove before continuing on to Henscath and Mullion Cliff. The cliffs at Pedn-y-ke are exposed to marine erosion and weathering, and although there are small areas of these cliffs which show evidence of working this was probably for copper or iron. There is no evidence of soapstone. There was however one uneconomic mid 19th century Copper mine called Wheal Fenwick a short distance inland to the south east of Pollurian Cove.(41)

In 1752 Crisp and Sanders had a 10 year licence at Mullion Cliffs but this time they paid a Guinea (£1- 1s) for the first 20 tons and the sum of 15 shillings per ton for every ton over 20 tons. A record in the agents rough account book located some years previously at Lanhydrock shows that on 14th November 1752 a total of 29 tons and 12 cwts of clay was weighed out from Mullion and a cash payment of £28.3s.6d was paid by Nicholas Crisp.(42)

This may have been the full total produced from the Mullion Quarry in the first year and this would have easily surpassed the minimum quota showing that prospects at this time were good. In the absence of first hand accounts of the mining the Licences do provide some information about mining activity. In these instances the miners working for Crisp and Sanders had to weigh up at least every 2 months in the presence of the landlords agent or steward, who had to be given at least 3 days notice.

They were committed to mine, *"Effectually with a sufficient number of men at all times in the year after the best manner for finding and raising the soapyrock... and at the end thereof will quietly leave and yield up into the hands of Mary Hunt ...without removing or taking out of the said mines and premises any timber planks or other supports Fixed placed or sett in the premises..."*

In 1758, after 6 years of running this Licence, Sanders died leaving Crisp to carry on the business. He suffered serious financial difficulties allegedly involving the misuse of pension funds in London which resulted in his bankruptcy, and in 1763 all the stock was sold up. He moved to a pottery at Bovey Tracey experimenting with materials on behalf of William Cookworthy. His experiments with local materials were unsuccessful and he again went into debt and was eventually imprisoned. This again shows how difficult it was to master not only the art of porcelain making, but more especially running a successful business. It was therefore a significant business achievement for Lund and especially the Worcester partners to be so successful.(42)

Both the Crisp and Sanders Licences involved cliff quarrying. There is an interesting reference within this licence to wooden structures erected and used by the miners to assist them to remove the soaprock and it is likely that wooden "scaffolding", chutes, and winches would have been erected in the quarried areas due to the location of the soaprock in the cliff face. In relation to Caerthillian, early Gew Graze, and Mullion the proximity of the soaprock to the sea and the effect of the high tides would have made this essential. There is evidence at Caerthillian Cliffs of what may have been a rock platform cut into the cliffs from which to work the now worked out soapstone veins. Directly above the quarries and visible from the coastal path, a footprint of a building exists, now grassed over with the stone reused in the field boundary walls. This could have been the site where the soaprock was sorted.

Details of accounts are not easy to locate, but can provide a meaningful description of day to day events.

From an Agents rough account book of the Robartes Lanhydrock Estate, held at the Courtney Library Collection in Truro the following entries appear, one of which includes the name of Nicholas Crisp.(42)

1752 16th October By cash from John Pascoe Lord Falmouths steward for your part of the clay dug out of the soapy rock at Lezard and weighed off in August last. £4-8s-11.1/2d (£4.45p)

14th November By cash from Nicholas Crisp esq for 29tons & 12 cwts of clay dug out of the soapyrock in Mullion and weighed in August last.£28.3s.6d (£28-17 1/2p)

1753 11th May By cash from John Pascoe Lord Falmouths steward for your part of the clay dug out of the soapy rock at Lizard and weighed off the 14th and 15th days of January last £4.14s.8d (£4.73p)

RICHARD CHAFFERS

In 1746-7 Richard Chaffers, an earthenware potter took over premises at Shaws Brow in Liverpool. The industry in Liverpool consisted of small factories, often with different family members working at different factories, and with itinerant workers and decorators. He became interested in producing a soft paste porcelain, and in 1754 he set up one of the earliest porcelain factories in Liverpool making a greyish soft paste ware which was decorated with Chinese scenes in blue on white. He was a popular man in Liverpool, who was influenced by Wedgwoods high standards. Although Wedgwood did not use soapstone, Chaffers decided to change direction and to manufacture china made from soapstone.

In 1755 he was visited by Richard Podmore, who had left Worcester and taken the soaprock secret with him, contrary to his earlier contract promise. The story may have been somewhat romanticised, no doubt being retold many times.

Entrance to soapstone working on west side of Sandy Vro

Worcester	Chaffers	Christian	Christian

Rare 4¹/₂" tea pot 1754   *Jumping boy* tea bowl and saucer   Sauce boat 1775   Polychrome trio late 1760's

Exposed soapstone vein - Mullion Cove cliff

Soapstone vein on ledge - Mullion Cove

Torchlight Cave Mine - Worked out stope

THE SOAPROCK TRAIL

Pengersick *'Old Mullion'* Quay

Pengersick cliff - quarry trench

Soapstone drift working - Gew Graze beach

Site of Benjamis Lval quarry

Soapstone vein in Serpentine - Pentreath

2 Entrance to Torchlight Cave Mine

1 Mullion Cove

3 Penruddock Quarry

3 Escarpment at Penruddock Quarry

5 North side of Gew Graze showing location of Lund Quarries

6 Beach quarry at Pentreath

6 Pentreath/Caerthillian quarry sites

N

+ MULLION
Mullion Cove **1**
Meaver • Vean
The Vro **2** Tonkens Point
Penruddock
Predannack Head
3 Daroose
Wheal Foss
Predannack Downs
Ogo Dour
Vellan Head
Pengersick Cliff Quarry
Pengersick Quay
Pengersick Point **4**
Lund Quarries
Gew Graze **5**
Lizard Downs
Kynance Cove

SOAPROCK COAST
The Lizard peninsula
August 2011

Pentreath
Caerthillian Crofts **6**

Entrance to Torchlight Cave Mine

All soapstone porcelain images courtesy of a private collector

Vauxhall tea bowl/saucer 1755-60

Worcester sauce boat pre 1757

Caughley 'Gillyflower' plate c1780

Vauxhall mug 1755-60

Richard Podmore, having left Worcester, had intended to emigrate to America via Liverpool to manufacture porcelain but before leaving he visited Richard Chaffers. After a long discussion during which Chaffers was impressed by his knowledge, Podmore decided to join him in Liverpool, and try to compete with Wedgwood and the other Staffordshire Potteries by manufacturing Steatitic Porcelain using soaprock from Cornwall. In order to do so Chaffers needed to go to Cornwall in search of the soaprock, but the only available sources were taken and already licensed. He obtained letters of introduction from Lord Derby, Lord Strange and other notable men before riding by horse to Cornwall and *"having taken leave of his wife and numerous family and friends, mounted with a pair of saddlebags under him, containing a supply of linen, a 1000 guineas, the first instalment to pay the wages of the miners, a pair of pistols in his holsters, pursuing his journey to London".*(40)

He did not travel directly to Cornwall but instead he rode to Parliament in London to make approaches to several land owners on the Lizard , many of whom were serving MPs there. Whilst in London he sought and obtained permission to bore for soaprock in several areas of the Lizard. He was unable to obtain it from Gew Greaze as it was in the possession of the Worcester company, while Caerthillian was in the possession of Nicholas Crisp, and there was no where else known where soaprock could be found at that time. On arrival Chaffers straight away began to employ miners to search for soaprock. These miners would have been employed locally searching for copper and other minerals at local mines and ventures, many of which were short lived with only limited profitability. The searching process, we are told, was *"somewhat akin to the process of boring for coal in our country"*, which would obviously entail drilling in some form or creating numerous small pits in which to look for the soaprock.(40)

Initially he was unsuccessful and found the project arduous and very expensive. During the search he kept in contact with his wife in Liverpool by writing to her. Despite searching at length he reached the stage where he had to suspend the search and return to Liverpool. According to the story, he gathered his miners together to pay them up, but one miner was missing. He was told that he had gone off to search for soapstone in a different location. The mine captain was Gavregan Teppit. The story goes that Chaffers paid him the mans wages and began to leave. Unknown to Chaffers the miner had located a workable soapstone vein and was vainly attempting to attract his attention. Eventually the miner found Chaffers and the team of miners set about recovering the soapstone. *"He obtained an ample supply of the sought after clay which was conveyed to the nearest port and thence shipped to Liverpool."* It was reported that on the ships arrival in Liverpool people cheered and flags flew.(40)

Chaffers made his way back to Liverpool via London. On the way there he was taken ill, caused by the exertions of the excessive travel and the search, and was unable to continue to Liverpool. He was so ill he was unable to contact his wife and was forced to remain at an Inn where he was helped by a Physician who sent word to his wife. His recovery took several weeks and eventually he made his way back home where he began to produce his porcelain ware. By December 1756 he had proved to his own satisfaction that the porcelain had high thermal resistivity.

He was quick to advertise ; *"Chaffers and co China Manufactory. The porcelain or china ware, made by messrs Chaffers and Co, is sold nowhere in the town, but at their manufactory on Shaws Brow, considerable abatement for exportation, and to all wholesale dealers. N.B. All the ware is proved with boiling water before it is exposed for sale."* In a short time, he was producing good quality porcelain, so much so that he was able to present Wedgwood with a tea service drawing the comments from Wedgwood that .... *" This puts an end to the battle. Mr Chaffers beats us all in his colours and with his knowledge he can make colours for 2 guineas which I cannot produce so good for five"* Chaffers, with Podmore acting as foreman, went on to produce quality porcelain products for a number of years and achieved widespread acclaim.

Much of his work, which is said to resemble that of Worcester , and consisted of dinner services and some tea and coffee sets. Large amounts were exported to America and the West Indies.

The Licence Chaffers initially obtained to mine the soaprock was issued on 24th June 1756. It was granted by George Hunt of Lanhydrock to Richard Chaffers and partners to mine for soapyrock, *".... in the Goss Moor adjoining the Predannack Downs and from thence into the said Downs lying and being in the Parish of Mullion in the said County of Cornwall (that is to say) to work* on the said veins or loads from the tail of Wheal Providence adit from the north west to the work or mine called Wheal Providence* to the south east and to have 100 fathoms of ground on each side of the said adit to the North and South thereof for the term of 15 years ... provided that no notice is given in writing one half year before the end of the first and every other term of 3 years of the said term of fifteen years. Under the yearly rent of £31 10s for the first 30 tons and £1 1s for every other ton. The first years rent to be payable at Midsummer 1757."

*It appears that this mine was first known as Wheal Ghostcroft in 1724. It was closed and reopened on several occasions by different groups of Adventurers, and during this time was also named as Wheal Unity, South Wheal Unity, the Mullion Mine, Predannack Wartha Mine, Wheal Trenance, as well as Wheal Providence.(42a) The last reported reference to the mine being "worked" for copper in the 18th century was in 1754 when surface spoils were searched for copper and weighed in by the owner Hugh Tonken.(42a) In 1757 a licence was issued to Tonken to mine for copper on the old adits but little work was done as he died in 1760.

The shafts were not used again for copper until about 1810 when they were reopened as Wheal Unity.

Information from the Soapstone Licence about adits would indicate that the area worked on behalf of Chaffers was an underground Mine, and close to part of the older copper works. The malleable copper ore, was known to be associated with Soapstone or steatite veins. The soaprock mine or mines were in the Predannack Wartha, on land close to the adits of Wheal Providence. There was a requirement to take at least 20 tons per year over and above the first 30 tons meaning a commitment to take 50 tons (50 metric tons) per year.

This and other Licences show that the Landowners were keen to retain all their mining rights from what essentially were resources of unknown potential and therefore maximise any income, but at the same time preserve the income from agricultural land. The search for soaprock would have continued in all areas bounded by the Licences and it is likely that many small scale units were started and abandoned if they were not productive enough, or more likely converted to stone quarries.

RICHARD CHAFFERS ... MULLION AND THE GAVREGAN TEPPIT LETTERS TO RICHARD CHAFFERS IN LIVERPOOL

In the 19th Century extracts from a series of letters written by Gavregan Teppit to Richard Chaffers in Liverpool were published. Teppit was employed by Chaffers to manage the quarrying and mining of the soaprock in Mullion. The original letters covered a period of eleven years, from July 1756 to December 1767 but their current whereabouts are unknown. The letters show that Chaffers was obtaining soaprock in Mullion in large quantities, and this took place well before William Cookworthy was experimenting with China Clay for his hard paste porcelain.

Extracts from these letters published in the 19th Century provide helpful day to day information about the running of the Quarries and Mines.(40) See below.

1756 9th July Teppit speaks of Chaffers having recently left Mullion and he hopes the drawing would answer the charges; He had set some men to work, and paid their wages,and was in good order for raising the clay, and had raised 2 tuns or thereabouts
1756 2nd October He will send about 10 tuns of clay, but was afraid of a disturbance between the Lords of the Land when he weighed it off. His "charges out of this present was not much up or down of £13" He sends his compliments to Mr Podmore.
1756 22nd November Teppit says he had sent to "Hail (Hayle) 8 tuns and 14 hundred (cwt) of sopey rock". He had put it into casks with directions upon each sort. During 1757 and 1758 they were still raising soaprock in the summer months and shipping it to Liverpool.
1759 August 26th "We are going on well with the sopey rock and have placed tackle over the plate and have a very good prospick of cleay now in sight and hope we shall gaine sume of your large charges that is past.

1759 November 9th *"We have the finest parcel of Clay that was ever found in Penradock."*

1759 Dec 8th *Teppit had weighed of the clay 9 tons and 17 hundred of as nice a clay as has ever been seen, and said that there was a man down in October who said he would give any money for such a parcel.*

1760 February 8th *" I hope we shall raise this summer so much as we did laste. We began in April and gave over in November."*

1760 Aug 9th *" We are going on very well upon the sopeyrock, hope to hear the last parcel of clay arrived safe and well, will send ten tun in the next.*

1761 March *" I have sent the clay to Hail firmly caskt up. We are obliged to shout night an day and pouder is dear. The cost of everything from 1st March 1760 to March 1761 is £94.*

1761 May 23rd *"We have found a very good bunch of clay, if it holds we can rise two or three hundred (weight) a day, and when the level is in, I hope it will serve for many years"*

1762 Sept 9th *"We raise half a tun of a day".*

1763 June 25th *"The quarterly charges are about £20 . The place is worth a hundred pound in sight now more than it was laste year, for we have a deep adit in and we are rising of clay faste"*

1763 July 14th *Teppit sends 12 tons of clay.*

1763 Aug 20th *He sends ten tuns of sopey rock*

1763 Oct 5th *Sends of 10 tons more in 35 casks. In 1764 the soap-rock yields well and is duly shipped via Hail to Liverpool.*

Mathematicians will note that the weight of each cask would be approximately 720lbs (or 326.5Kg)

CHAFFERS MINE

There is a record by AK Hamilton Jenkin referring to the area of the Richard Chaffers Soapstone Licence in which he records that the grant (Licence) covers practically the same area as that of the Wheal Providence and South Wheal Unity mines and writes that, *"Whilst the exact site of Chaffers later working is not known, it undoubtedly lay in the same vicinity. The letters of Gavregan Teppit who was in charge of Chaffers operations from 1756-1767 suggest that part of the 'clay' as he calls it, may even have been won from the adit of South Wheal Unity; at all events it was obtained by underground mining. Throughout the correspondence Teppit makes reference to 'levels', and to the use of gunpowder, explaining that they were forced to shoot (i.e 'blast') night and day. In 1763 he writes "We have a deep adit in and are rising of clay fast" and elsewhere "We have the finest parcel of clay that was ever found in Penradock. In 1766, a year after Chaffers death, Teppit stated, that whilst their grant was confined to the winning of clay they had recently struck into some copper-works" wherein they found ore worth £96/ton, which implies that it must almost have been pure copper."(42a)*

This implies that there may be at least one unidentified shaft other than the original copper mine shafts in the vicinity of Wheal Providence, and that the scale of operations was much wider than previously thought with a number of sites both above and underground in operation at the same time.

In the 20th century a lot of levelling and clearance work was done in the vicinity of the mine from the upper site down to the lower section through the valley which runs north west feeding the site of the old Creiggian (Criggan) Mill complex in the lower reaches. Part of this levelling and clearance work is believed to have involved moving spoil to help construct the wartime Predannack airfield. There are remains of an old track road running up the eastern side of this valley in the direction of the Mine adits. This disappears close to the footpath which runs across the edge of the Downs. This is the path which can be traced down to the old straight footpath which heads from Predannack Wartha towards the tower of Mullion Church in the distance and which can still be followed through fields 200 yards south east of Trenance and into the village. Local information suggests the possibility of at least one deep underground void here other than in the area close to the mine adit described by Hamilton Jenkin.

On the western side of the valley are some overgrown remains of an old zig-zag cart trackway or lane cut into the hillside. This is distinguishable from the "firebreak" cut into the vegetation because it shows short lengths of path which have been cut into the hillside exposing sections of bedrock. Underfoot as it progresses down the hillside to join the lane by the old Mill. This appears to follow the route of the lane shown on the old Victorian survey map and was no doubt the cart route used from Predannack Wartha to the Harbour. Much of this land which formed part of the area worked by Chaffers has been altered as one would expect since the 1750s but it provided many tons of soapstone for the porcelain factory in Liverpool.

In 1765 Richard Podmore was taken ill with "a malignant fever, without hope of recovery". Chaffers was asked to visit him, but this proved to be a fatal mistake for Chaffers as he also contracted the fever and subsequently died in December 1765. Both Podmore and Chaffers were eventually buried close together in St. Nicholas Graveyard in Liverpool. The last letter sent to Richard Chaffers is dated 26th November 1765 and contains an account of all the monies received and paid by Teppit up to that date. The porcelain industry in Liverpool didnt fully recover and many of his potters and decorators emigrated to America, or went to work for Wedgwood and other companies in Staffordshire.(40)

In December 1765 Richard Chaffers died and the balance was transmitted in January 1766 by Hannibal Chaffers .

The work continued in Mullion and on January 29th, 1766 Teppit wrote to Hannibal saying he has 20 tons to weigh off, and a very good vein in sight. They had also located some good deposits of copper which were making £96 a ton. He finished by saying that *"As for your lease, no one shall see it without your orders"*. It is understood that a seperate Licence was required and was actually obtained to mine the copper. The document, being a combined lease traced by Sonia Parkinson.

1766 Feb 27th Teppit wrote to Edward Chaffers and his Executors,Administrators and Assigns, and to pay one pound of lawful money per ton to the Lords when the clay is weighed off. Mr Christian has desired me to send him the account of what cash I received from Mr R Chaffers , which I have done to the best of my knowledge as follows- received from May 1756 to February 1766 - £730.6s. 3d. (£730.32p). (40)

The last letter of the series addressed to Mr Edward Chaffers is dated December 10th 1767 when the works were still in operation in Mullion. Phillip Christian, Hannibal Chaffers and Edward Chaffers became executors and took over the business, completing the purchase in 1771.(40)

THE USE OF GUNPOWDER IN THE 18TH CENTURY

One of the most interesting feature of these extracts is the costly use of gunpowder to extract the soapstone from the bedrock. This does help to answer a question often asked about the quarries and while not all the soapstone required removal by explosive it may provide an explanation as to why the workforce appeared to be so small in comparison to other types of quarrying and mining activity. Early use of gunpowder in

Mullion Cliff Quarry

18th century drift (B) Mullion Cove

Wide soapstone vein
Porth Pyg cliff face

quarrying and mining was widespread, yet it was one of the most dangerous of occupations. It frequently resulted in accidents,deaths and maiming of the men. In the 18th century it involved the boring of a 1" cylindrical hole in the rock, 2 or more feet in depth, using an iron instrument similar to a cold chisel which is held by one miner while another hit it with a mallet. The hole was flushed clean with water. The gunpowder was often introduced from a common flask, the amount introduced was often a matter of guesswork resulting in excess having to be removed with a wet reed. A "cartridge" was made of paper, filled with gunpowder and cemented with candle tallow. This was then pushed into the hole with an iron needle or bar often releasing the powder which had then to be pushed back into the hole. The hole was then covered with clay or oakum (tarred fibre), a hole passed through with a 2 foot long skewer and a charge of rolled quills introduced all of which was tightly rammed together filling any hole with brick or stone. A solid arch was formed over the charge to retain the blast and a tamping bar used to ram it tighter and the charge was then fired.(43) Teppit reported that gunpowder was being used *"day and night"* in 1761. Mullion would have become a noisy place to live.

By 1800 the Cornish mining and quarrying industries were consuming 4000 barrels of gunpowder per annum, none of which was manufactured in Cornwall at that time. The first Cornish Gunpowder factory opened up in 1808 and was at Perran-ar-Worthal, 5 miles from Falmouth.(43a) Gunpowder (made by grinding charcoal, sulphur and saltpetre together)was believed to have been first used in Cornish mines at Godolphin in 1689 but a safety fuse was not developed until 1830 by William Bickford-Smith, who in 1874 bought the Trevano Estate near to Helston. He utilised a thin rope filled with gunpowder and sealed with gum to create a slow even burning fuse which was to save hundreds of lives in the mining industry.(43a)(43b)

In the 1990s Sonia Parkinson located a previously unidentified Licence issued in July 1772 to Philip Christian and son relating to Predannack Woollas. The existence of this licence was known about for many years and erroneously referred to in Victorian textbooks by Binns and Harvey as being sold to Worcester for £500. This shows how difficult it is to trace, locate, view and interpret all the information about the soapstone quarrying and mining industry on the Lizard. It shows that there were 6 men involved in the lease to Christian, Thomas Vyvyan the elder of Kestle,Thomas Vyvyan the younger of Trewan,Hugh Lyne of the Parish of Mawgan of Meneage, Oliver Oliver of Polteshaw (Poltesco?) in the parish of Grade, John Nicholas in the Parish of Cury and Thomas Roskilly of the Parish of Mullion. Christian was granted full and free liberty licence and authority to dig mine work and search for clay or soapy rock …. in and upon all and every such veins or loads of soapstone … now discovered or shall hereinafter discover throughout all or any part of the Manor of Predannack Woollas in the Parish of Mullion. The term was for 21 years , an annual rental payment of 10 guineas whether they mined or not plus a payment of a guinea for every ton once it was "spalled, washed, dressed, made merchantable and weighed off". Three days notice of weighing off was required. There was a further unusual provision in that if the Christians discovered tin,copper or copper ore while driving or working the soapy rock then if the Christians applied within 2 months to the grantors then they would be given the right to mine and sell the metals for a 21 year period. The grantors were to take one sixth of a share of any tin, copper or other metals. This Licence was sold to Worcester in 1776 for £500.(30b)

The implication of this Licence is that there was an extension of the area which could be searched and quarried for soapstone or more licences. The soapstone lies within the Serpentine boundaries. There are no known large soapstone quarries as a result of this Licence but there is an indication that the serpentine boundaries do extend into Predannack Woollas land. The coastal margin of the serpentine includes The Vro and runs south west of Penruddock close to Predannack Wartha village, then south east towards Predannack Woollas, missing the coastal strip by Ogo Dour, turning south about 100 yards from the cliff edge and includes the cliffs leading in the direction of Vellan Head. There are two small elongated strips of Serpentine about 200 yards west of Ogo Dour which border the sea, but no old work is visible. There is no more serpentine west of this line, but it is found right across the Lizard in an easterly direction.

11. The Mullion Cove soaprock working

On first examination Mullion Cove does not present itself as being part of an historical industrial environment.

Early records and evidence about the methods of soapstone quarrying and mining activities which took place in the area are mainly restricted to letters sent by Gavregan Teppit to his employer Richard Chaffers in Liverpool.

The Cove was first worked by Crisp and Sanders in 1752 when the land was owned by Mary Hunt of Lanhydrock. In 1756 Richard Chaffers and Phillip Christian of Liverpool were certainly associated with the area working inland from the cliffs near to the Wheal Providence Mine. Other coastal areas of Cornwall, such as Tintagel had cliff workings on a large scale several hundred years earlier. The Soapstone Licence issued at that time covered the whole length of the Mullion Cliffs, the "Harbour area" and south Henscath, and also north to Pedyn-y-ke which borders Pollurian Beach. No soapstone was found north of Henscath.

It should be noted that in 1750 the sea level may well have been lower than at the present time, and this is important for the quarrying and mining of the soapstone, much of which in the 18th Century was conducted on the cliffs and beaches, in particular at Gew Graze and Mullion Cove. Recent academic work has shown that by using available tidal records and observational evidence it can be shown that global sea level (GSL) has risen sharply since the late 18th Century by at least 10 inches(25cms).(44) Even with a lower sea level it would not have been easy to work from the Cove beach.

The effects of sea level changes was more immediate on the 1st November 1755. A great earthquake struck the Portuguese city of Lisbon, creating a tsunami which reached Cornwall. About 6 hours after the earthquake struck the sea rose suddenly in the early afternoon creating a series of large waves which lasted over two hours. At St Michaels Mount the sea level rose suddenly and retired. Ten minutes later it rose by six feet (1.8m) very rapidly, then ebbed rapidly. At Penzance the sea rose eight feet (2.4m) and even higher at Newlyn. Large boulders weighing six to eight tonnes were swept along like pebbles. It was observed by the likes of William Borlase and would no doubt have effected the men, had they been quarrying at Mullion.(44a)(47)

Older local residents in the village can still recall that in their childhood days they could still regularly walk around the harbour wall at low tide to access the Cove Beach but such walks around the harbour wall are now rare. A black and white photograph taken around 1890 lent to me by a village resident has provided a lot of comparative information about the Cove and I have used it in this book as a comparison. Many people will find it difficult and somewhat unusual to discover that only 140 years before this photograph was taken the cove was the scene of industrial quarrying and mining. Even at that time, much of that history seems to have been forgotten.

The photo was taken from the Henscath Cliff, below the current Mullion Cove Hotel, almost exactly the same view as that taken today by hundreds of visitors each year. The

Cut ledge B

Serpentine promontary leading to Torchlight Cave

Entrance to Torchlight Cave showing soapstone

MULLION COVE circa 1890

Photograph courtesy of a Mullion resident

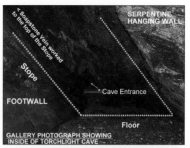

Inside Cave Mine plan

Extremity of mine working

Unworked soapstone pillar

scene looks south, before the building of the southern pier of the Harbour in the late 19th century and shows most of the Cove looking towards Porth Pyg high cliff. Although it may have been taken at a very low tide it does show that the beach seems much more extensive than today. The serpentine cliffs in the Cove in the 1700s were, and still are unstable, but surprisingly the location of substantial veins of soapstone are still visible.

A general examination of the cliffs today is possible at low tide or by using binoculars. Access to the Cove is gained from the current harbour foreshore through a narrow cave, approximately 25 yards (23m) in length. It is an old cave which drew the attention of writers in Victorian times. A visitor passing through to the beach today needs to be careful where he put his feet but in the gloom, with the aid of a good torch or a camera flash one can still see remains of the red and green serpentine rock lining the walls of the cave... and the remains of a soapstone vein in the roof.

The Rev. Johns in his book "A week at the Lizard" published in 1848, wrote the following, " *Mullion Cove should be visited about mid day on the second or third day after new or full moon. The tide is then low, and several interesting spots may be inspected which at other times are inaccessible. The rocks on both sides are very beautiful; that on the left is perforated by a natural archway many yards long, leading to an open part of the shore, which near the base of the cliff is covered with huge blocks of stone, and further out is composed of firm sand. No time should be lost in traversing this and traversing a projecting mass of serpentine, for on the other side of it lies the entrance to, by far, the most imposing of those caves on the coast which are accessible from the land. There can be no doubt that at some very distant period it was filled up by lodes of soft steatite which has since been worn away by the action of the sea."(45)*

There is little doubt that this so called "natural archway", was an early worked soapstone Drift which cuts right through the serpentine promontory into the Cove. In fact there is another partially cut one adjacent to it next to the Harbour walkway which can be entered and the remains of the soapstone can be seen in the roof of the cut. There are similarities with soapstone workings further along the cove which have only recently been investigated and will be discussed later.

Soapstone veins in Porth Pyg Quarry

Through the cave or tunnel there is an oval topped opening to the left which, over the years has been visited by hundreds of people. The outline of this cave makes its origin something which has been under speculation for some time. A copy of a water colour painting by the Rev. F.C. Jackson, former Victorian vicar of Ruan Minor, shows an "artists" view of the bay painted from this cave at low tide, and one which is still recognisable today.(4) I have begun this section with a description of the Cove during the 19th Century, in order to explain that life 260 years ago was far different from that of today and to say that the Cove itself, with no harbour piers or shelter went through a period when human industrial activity would have had a significant impact on the coastal and rural activities of the people who lived in this area.

Drift A adjacent to Cove Quarry

MULLION COVE QUARRIES, ADITS, DRIFTS, TUNNELS AND LEDGES

Hamilton Jenkin wrote that, *"in Porth Pyg, south of Mullion Harbour several short tunnels have been driven in the cliff on what appear to be veins of steatite and that a somewhat longer level could be seen near the Vro Rock".*(46)

This is one of few references to mining or industrial activity in the Cove but its significance to the history of soapstone workings does not seem to have been either recognised or remembered since. About 80 yards to the south of the Harbour is a towering cliff face at least 100 foot high. It is best viewed from the beach itself or from a small boat. Beneath the cliff face are sections of steep rocky scree, which run down to the beach where there are massive serpentine boulders weighing many tons. In this open rock face are veins of soapstone. The rock scree is mainly composed of weathering angular pieces of serpentine along with smaller pieces of soapstone which have fallen or been worked from the veins in the cliff face overhanging the site. This is the site of the one of the 18th Century Mullion Cliff Quarries from which many tons of soapstone and hundreds of tons of rock have been removed. Adjacent to the quarry, and probably associated with it is a small tunnel (Drift 1) cut into the cliff just above the high water mark. It is about 6 foot high, 3-4 foot wide and is worked into the serpentine for a distance of approximately 15 yards. It is cut between two narrow veins of soapstone.

Upper worked area

Because of a roof fall it is not possible to find the true depth of this drift but it does turn slightly south as if to run behind the scree slope. An old local explanation for this Drift suggests that it was associated with drainage from the copper mine approximately a mile away but this is unlikely due to the nature of other similar small Drifts in the Cove connected to the soapstone working.

The oldest documentary reference to the copper mine is at Wheal Ghostcroft in 1741. Hamilton Jenkin wrote *"... found in a deed dated 20th September 1741 in which the Revd. Hugh Tonken, Vicar of Mullion and Walter Reed of Stithians were granted liberty to dig and search for copper ore and other minerals on a copper lode called Wheal Providence in Predannack Wartha Commons and Croft adjoining wherein is an adit already begun. In 1742 a grant was made to Henry Harris of Gwennap and William Passmore of Helston defining the limits of the sett as 70 fathoms of ground on the run of the lode ... in the Croft of Goon Vean which is to begin from the cliffs ... with liberty to drive on the adit end to the next pitch or grant, in case it should be thought fit to drive from the adit end that is now driving. A subsequent lease dated 24th May 1748, empowered the driving of "a new adit into the said old copper work. In November 1754 when dues were paid by Tonken for copper gotten out of the burrows in the Mullion Mine"*. The statement suggests that underground operations had ceased by that date.(46)

Henscath Cliff Quarry

Apparently the limits of the sett were to begin at the cliffs, not the adit itself. The burrows are spoil heaps of excavated material raised from an adjacent shaft.

Reed was a successful and experienced tin miner, mine manager and speculator in West Cornwall, while Tonken was Mullion's vicar and a co investor with mining interests.

A promontory of serpentine at the south end of the Cove called "Tonkens Point" was named after him. It is likely that the copper workings started before 1742 and may have begun as "Ghost Mine" around 1724.(48)

Henscath soapstone vein

According to Hamilton Jenkin, the mine was served by 2 adits, one about 7 fathoms deep and the other just over 20 fathoms deep. The former adit was used as a water supply which followed the tributary of a stream running down the valley to the old Mill at Criggan.

The deeper one was believed to have been dug in the 1740s and reportedly began in the cliff, possibly from the Vro, but Hamilton Jenkin was of the opinion that it followed the line of the shallower adit towards the harbour, but was deeper. There appears to be little working of the copper from the late 1750s until the early 1800's, which initial date curiously enough coincides with the commencement of the soapstone quarries and mines and may indicate that they turned completely from mining copper to quarrying soapstone.

Rev. Jackson watercolour (4)

The men would have been sure of being paid and they had tools, equipment, the knowledge to adapt, and certainly enough material to excavate for many years. The enthusiasm of the porcelain potters to obtain the soapstone was evident from an early period. The drifts in the Cove at Mullion are identical to similar ones found around the Cornish coast cut in the 18th Century, where mining activity has taken place. Their design was sufficient enough to allow access and working by one man and a wheelbarrow.(49)

According to the letters of Gavregan Teppit to Richard Chaffers in March 1761 we know that gunpowder was regularly used to break up the rock in order to obtain the soapstone. This was not uncommon in the 18th Century but was a very dangerous procedure and may have been in use in the cliffs before that time.

It would seem from the letters that there were small groups of miners, 4-5 in number at work on a particular local site, but evidence of the extent of the workings would now suggest a much bigger working community involving both men and women. In common with similar enterprises it is likely that the soapstone was initially worked by men lowered down the cliff face in skips from fixed ropes at the top of the cliff. They may have had to change the lie of the cliff by using gunpowder to create a more vertical work area in which to use the equipment and cradles. Information about the practicalities of removing the soapstone prior to sorting are not to be found in the remaining letters currently available, but it would be probably being raised in buckets or containers and taken to a sorting area , isolated from the serpentine and loaded into casks, before being weighed and shipped.

This may help strengthen evidence suggesting the soapstone was first raised to the cliff top and shipped by horse and cart down to the sorting area using the old tracks which existed. Some old tracks did in fact run towards the top of the cliffs. The soapstone at this location is the pale green variety, and there are several forms, which appear to depend on the degree of weathering of the serpentine. Some are hard and brittle like "flint" when first exposed to the air but soon break up into small blocks when the moisture is removed. Others are already weathered and exhibit bright green/pale blue colouration similar to residual copper staining. This also disintegrates to a powder when dried or crushed. This was the soapstone material so sought after, which helped the potters stop the porcelain from "flying", that is crack, craze or break when hot water was added to the finished product. Because soapstone quarrying was so rare there are few references to the methods used and certainly the section of coast at Caerthillian, Gew Graze and Mullion are the only such areas known to have been worked in this way in the country.

Working at Mullion Cove was regarded as dangerous due to the unstable nature of the serpentine bedrock. About 120 yards further along the Cove from the Quarry towards the south west is a second tunnel, identically cut Drift 2 is also just above the High Water Mark. The Drift is cut directly between 2 veins of soapstone, the lower of which being 12" wide was subsequently removed at the foot of the cliff by driving a small tunnel into the vein at right angles to create a small cavern which was worked. This is no doubt one of the features described by Hamilton Jenkin. With the use of hammers, bars and chisels this allowed a greater volume of mineral to be removed. Such was the demand, and the allowances of the Licences, there was quarrying activity in the Cove wherever the soapstone was accessible.

The soapstone at Drift 2 is a grey/green in colour, hard when in the vein but crumbles easily when broken off and dried. This method would only have yielded relatively small tonnage and removal would have been affected by tidal activity. It should be remembered that what is seen today are only the remnants of the soapstone which was worked 250 years ago when sources would have been much larger and veins wider. Above Drift 2 there is a small serpentine promontory which turns south east. Some 80 yards further along the rocky beach is the semi circular high cliff of Porth Pyg. Today part of this high cliff slope is covered by a steep rocky scree which was not present in the late 19th Century, as can be shown by the old black and white 1890 photograph. Much of todays scree has disintegrated and fallen in the last 5 years.

It should be noted that Cornish Serpentine cliffs are often unstable and before going on I would like to remind the reader of a paradox recorded by Rev. Johns in 1848 (p141) concerning cliff exploration ... *"It is much more difficult to descend than to ascend the face of a precipitous cliff, and therefore less dangerous; and again it is much easier to ascend a place of the same character than to descend, and therefore more dangerous".(45)* Those of us who have already tried it will know that it is true.

Additional activity is visible around the edge of the bay above the high water mark, with the creation of 2 ledges one on the eastern side of the bay which is about 60 yards long and one on the south side which is about 30 yards in length. I have called these ledges simply Ledge A and Ledge B and they can be viewed on the photographs.

Anyone walking the cliff path can see them clearly from above The base of the ledges follows the path of a vein of pale green soapstone 1-2 foot in width and both run towards the bottom of the Porth Pyg high cliff near to todays large scree deposit. It appears that the existence of the ledges being above the High Water Mark also allowed the working of a single vein of soapstone about one foot wide almost around the whole of this section of the cliffs. The soapstone is visible today, and in parts provides not only the green material but also the much sought after white. It is possible that the ledges were created as an attempt to work a single vein about 1-2 foot wide almost right around the bay above the high water mark and in doing so created a path part way around the Cove which was wide enough to walk on as well as allow the use of a wheelbarrow.

It is suggested that these ledges also provided access routes to and from a second Quarry in the corner of the Cove below Porth Pyg High Cliff still visible today. In other words it appears that this area was another quarry, marked as Quarry 2. The ledge is between 6 - 10 foot (2 - 3 metres) wide in parts, with one part of Ledge B which has an abundance of white soapstone as wide as 15 to 20 foot.(4.5m-6m) The ledges would have been worked back into the cliff face for soapstone while the serpentine overburden would be discarded or reused in the countryside. Ledge A runs north to south for about 60 yards and today has large boulders blocking it which have fallen from the cliff above. It is not easily accessible but can be viewed from above. Ledge B runs East to West for about 30 yards, around the front of a larger serpentine outcrop,and is accessible today by a short climb at low tide from the beach onto the flat ledge. This ledge appears to end at the outer edge of the second serpentine promontory, but even here there is a much wider vein of worked soapstone. These veins are of soft pale green and white soapstone. Below this ledge is a second tunnel driven into the cliff perpendicular to a soapstone vein, again as described by Hamilton Jenkin. This vein and tunnel goes much deeper into the serpentine, about 15 yards, and opens up a worked area many times larger than the first tunnel.

This area can only be accessed at low tide.

In May 2011, due to the low tides, it was possible to walk around this promontory and access a location known locally as Torchlight Cave.

TORCHLIGHT CAVE

At the southern end of the Cove is a cave entrance hidden from the harbour. It is visible only from the sea, and is no doubt the one referred to by Johns in 1848 when he wrote, *"It is now a huge chink between two sombre rocks, the entrance being partially blocked up by a smooth black pillar curved like the cut-water of a ship. It is a striking object when seen externally, yet the view from within it is yet more so – impenetrable gloom above – streaming in through the fissures – but revealing nothing behind – the smoothest of all possible sands ... richly dark rocks ... St Michaels Mount in the extreme distance".(45)*

Google Earth ariel view Cove/Vro

North East side Sandy Vro

Soft soapstone clay

Today the sea encroaches some distance into the "Cave", and access to the entrance can only be gained on foot at low tide or by small boat in calm conditions. Locally this cave has long been known as "Torchlight Cave", and according to the Rev. Harvey it was the home of the "old fisherman Sam Hitchens with his bundle of furze and tar dipped torch to lighten up its innermost recesses." Sam Hitchens did in fact have a wife and family in the cove!(4)

The entrance to the cave faces west, out to sea, in the direction of Tonkens Point. The entrance has a large upright slightly angled pillar of blackened serpentine. This is some 25 foot (7.6m) high and separates two openings above which there are wide soapstone veins running almost vertically. At the entrance the soapstone appears to have fallen or been removed to ground level. To the northern or left hand side is a third smaller opening, which looks to have been originally driven in as a small drift in order to access and remove soapstone. It is just wide enough for one man to enter and opens out into a small cavern.

The main entrance tunnel, is also the entrance to the cave referred to by Johns in 1848, when he wrote "… There can be no doubt that at some very distant period it was filled up of loads of soft steatite which has since been worn away by the action of the sea."

The fact that Rev. Johns was able to get access to this cave at all would indicate that tides were lower in 1848, and even lower in the 1700s, a fact which anyone who tries to walk there now will recognise and appreciate. His speculation is surprising considering that it was only just over 60 years since the end of soapstone extraction in the Cove.

The main entrance is very similar in appearance to a similar smaller soapstone working visible in the intertidal area on Gew Graze beach where a small drift has been worked through steeply inclined veins of soapstone. Inside the entrance is an ante chamber about 40 foot(12m) in length. It is cavernous, with serpentine and soapstone in veins of different sizes, but with massive angular boulders on the sandy floor and two openings in the roof allowing light to enter, which may indicate an earlier roof fall. It then turns south into what initially appears to be a black void but when illuminated by torchlight is shown to be a grand serpentine cavern rather than just a cave.

The cave is 160 foot (48.8m)in length with a maximum roof height from the sandy floor of 45 foot (14m). The sand filled floor of the tunnel is about 12 foot(3.66m) wide, narrowing and sloping upwards by approximately 6 foot (1.8m)at the farthest end away from the sea. The outstanding feature in this cave is a steeply rising sloping bed of flat serpentine dipping steeply from west to east, which can only be described in hardrock mining terms as a stope or worked surface. At the top of the stope are the remains of a wide vein of soapstone.

STOPING

A stope is an excavated area produced during the removal of ore bearing rock. Often narrow, deep and elongated , it reflects the former position of the lode. A description of a Stope and Stoping is highly relevant to the process by which the soapstone has been extracted as it appears to typify the way much of the material was obtained,

Unnamed cove between Tonkens Point and Sandy Vro (SV1)

Drift entrance (DSV1)

Worked soapstone stope from DSV1 to DSV2 at Sandy Vro

particularly in the Mullion Cove location.. Stoping could be conducted in two ways. The first was where the vein would be extracted from the floor of the mine gallery by working downwards, with the "deads", or hand sorted rubbish being thrown up onto stemples, wooden arched platforms above the miners heads. This is called "underhand stoping."

Alternatively the ore or vein could be cut from the roof of the gallery, by driving upwards with the rubbish falling to the ground to be removed from the miners feet. This is called "Overhand stoping". The use of stoping produces voids which often have to be filled to prevent rock falls and roof falls onto the miners. In tin and copper mining there are voids which require backfilling or packing to provide support. The procedure was often used in conjunction with blasting, the use of gunpowder to remove the ore or mineral. The broken rock, or "deads" produced as a result of blasting can act as a working platform and assists the excavation by supporting the walls. The material produced is periodically removed. In soapstone mining here, the same principle would have applied, and it may have been assisted by blasting with powder, which is reported to have been occurring during the latter half of the 18th century. Stoping was used in Cornwall in the 17th and 18th centuries, with underhand stoping the most common in early Cornish mines. Overhand stoping however was less labour intensive, requiring less manpower to dispose of the "deads", less timber for storage, shorage etc and would require one long stope rather than several successive stages, and greater safety for the miners, particularly where the walls of the vein were unstable and stemples could not be securely fixed.(50)

Other advantages included that the ground breaks readily, the ore or vein can be thrown down, water drains away, ventilation is good, less timber is required.(51)

The Footwall of the stope in Torchlight cave dips approximately at 30 degrees to the east from the roof. The roof wall is called the Hanging Wall. There are the remains of a pale green soapstone vein which is almost 18 inches to two foot in thickness in places at the top of the stope. It is a rich vein which has no doubt been mined out by overhand stoping for the length of the tunnel and would have provided many tons of soapstone in the removal operation. Soapstone is the only visible mineral. There is no visible evidence, for example, of Copper ore.

The Hanging wall, rock removed in the extraction process appears to be made purely of serpentine. In a few sections of the Footwall, in particular at the farthest extremity, remnants of soapstone have been left in place and at the farthest point the roof seems to have a supporting pillar giving the impression of at least one chamber being cut. Chambers were regular features of hardrock mining because they created support. This last chamber is largely dry and above most of todays tides. It is large enough only for one man to have worked but it appears that most of the economically available soapstone has been removed.

Torchlight Cave, it is suggested, should be considered to be a small worked out stope of a soapstone mine rather than just a cave. The soapstone is of good quality and that remaining is still wet with groundwater turning it easily into a manageable clay. There is a small vertical gully about 6 inches wide cut into the Footwall of the stope about three quarters of the way along which may have been dug to allow groundwater or possibly even encroaching sea water to drain away.

There is also a small rock platform with roughly cut steps leading half way up the face, allowing access to a higher possibly later working level.

THE VRO ROCK

Because of the configuration of the cliffs in Mullion Cove, the entrance to Torchlight Cave is obscured and can only be seen from ground level or from the sea. About 300 yards to the south west, lying between Mullion Island and Torchlight Cave is a large natural serpentine rock island called "The Vro".

Following the steep cliffs about 90 yards south west, out from Torchlight Cave is a headland called Tonkens Point or Laden Ceyn. Between Tonkens Point and The Vro is another large serpentine promontory flanked by an unnamed cove to the north east and a cove called Sandy Vro to the South West. The photograph on page viii shows the small unnamed rocky cove which has been marked as, Cove SV1, followed by the unnamed point marked as Point T2 which is a serpentine promontory on the

Penruddock Quarry

Penruddock Escarpment

Lane to Wheal Foss and Daroose

eastern side of Sandy Vro. Sandy Vro, a local sandy beach used by villagers over a hundred years ago, was once accessible from the cliff top by a path but the lower end of the path has now disappeared into the sea.

It was also once regularly accessed by families and children in small boats put out from Mullion Harbour. Penruddock Soapstone Quarry is only 250 yards to the south east of the cliff top. The mouth of Cove SV1 is approximately 60 yards wide. At the base of the cliffs, about 100 yards from the mouth of the Cove can be seen a 1-2 foot wide pale green soapstone vein running almost vertically upwards for the full length of the cliff. At the foot of the vertical vein, the soapstone has been removed to a height of about 25 foot and there appears to have been a drive into the vein from ground level, now partly infilled, which stretches about 25 yards into the base of the cliff creating a deep cleft off which are small chambers apparently cut into the serpentine. Part of this has now been subjected to minor rock falls but inside there are areas which appear to have been hollowed out, in particular on the south west wall.

Part of the Thorneloe/Kempthorne Worcester porcelain service
Photo. Private collector

About 20 yards from the opening, also in the south west cliff face wall a horizontal Drift has been driven into the base of the cliff (DSV1). With its semi arched roof it is a 25 yard long tunnel, between the High and Low water marks, running perpendicular to a soapstone vein which dips steeply down from north west to south east, and visible along this cliff face. Inside the cut, the Drift has been developed and enlarged upwards to remove the soapstone vein to the north west creating a hanging wall, in an identical way to that found in Torchlight Cave, and elsewhere in the cove.

To the north west is the worked soapstone vein which has been cut back into the serpentine to form a footwall, removing about 30-40 feet of soapstone and part of the serpentine roof space.

From Sandy Vro beach on the opposite side of this headland is another soapstone vein which also dips into the beach level from the north west, with a 10 yard drive cut perpendicular to the vein (DSV2). The cut opens into a small cavern. The seaward side of the headland faces north west and there is a further 10 yard man made cut (DSV3), which joins this small cavern from an opening facing the sea. This cut continues straight into the promontory in a south easterly direction and joins with the first tunnel. The tunnels form a "dog leg" pattern which are three offset Drifts meeting from different directions.

On the south western side of Sandy Vro around the high tide mark is a small worked ledge of serpentine. There are some veins of grey white soapstone above and around the ledge which would indicate a level of past extraction. This area is some 350 yards from the harbour area and therefore would likely have been worked from above with access gained via the original path from Penruddock down to Sandy Vro. The soapstone was either removed from the sea cave to shallow boats or drawn up the cliff to the top in buckets. The shallow slope of the beach and tidal restrictions would have limited access by boats, so land access would have allowed quarrying for longer. In the small valley above Sandy Vro there does appear to be small grade infill material, the lower end of which has begun to disappear with higher tides. With the proximity of other quarries some of this infill may have been tipped there as spoil and helped upgrade the path or there may have been access to a winch here. There is a small amount of soapstone towards the south west of Sandy Vro which may have been partly removed, but the Vro marks the limit of the Serpentine and soapstone.

On the north side of Mullion Cove is an area on the south face of Henscath Cliff, between the west harbour pier and to the west side below the Cove "Cannon". The whole area shows signs of slippage today with open scree faces of smaller grade angular rocks. This is best seen from the cliffs on the opposite side of the Cove. Today there is evidence of small veins of white soapstone in the cliff face recently exposed on the western side of the cliff and on the eastern side by the footpath. These veins continue into the current harbour area and at the foot of Henscath Cliff is a particularly impressive 1 foot wide vein of pale green soapstone which appears to have been worked. It appears that the area above has been filled in with material of all grades and this may have come in part from the building of the Cove Hotel which is about 110 years old.

It is suggested that this was a third quarried area on the south side of the Henscath Cliff leading up behind the west wall of the harbour. There is also evidence of old iron mooring points on the bedrock no more than 10 yards from this large vein and two niches cut into the rock wall behind the ironwork. A 19th Century black and white photograph showing the building of the west harbour pier shows a distinctly defined quarry edge behind the harbour working, which could be indicative of the boundary.

Conversations with people who have developed land for building in vicinity of the Cove have revealed that no more than 3-4 foot (1-1/2m) below ground level there are still to be found significant deposits of soapstone which are several feet wide. In some cases these are the solid veins, whilst others are the soft clay-like veins similar to those originally found in Gew Graze. There is no evidence of any detriment to building on these sites.

The overal effect of investigation into Mullion Cove has resulted in the realisation that the whole of the Cove from Henscath right around to The Vro has been subjected to the extraction of soapstone from as early as 1752. This process of removal of soapstone from veins took place on an industrial scale using hard rock mining methods appropriate to the 18th century and especially by the use of overhand stoping. Open Quarrying took place on the cliff faces in the Cove and there was likely to be the use of gunpowder and blasting involved, both underground and on the surface.

At beach level, several perpendicular drifts have been driven into sharply dipping soapstone veins and worked internally for the mineral forming internal "cavities" of extraction. The Ledges were cut back to remove soapstone and probably to assist transport of rock and minerals from the quarries. Along with the examination of available Licences, it also suggests that there was an "Industrial Corridor of Extraction" covering an area from the Cove to Daroose and including Penruddock, Predannack Downs, and Wheal Foss, but it also incorporated the area around Wheal Providence (Unity) where Soapstone veins were known to exist in association with the Copper.

12. Widening the spread of the quarries.

The Porcelain Industry changed over the remainder of the 18th and early 19th Centuries resulting in a number of different names being associated with the quarrying and mining of the Soapstone.

PHILIP CHRISTIAN AND WILLIAM CHAFFERS OF LIVERPOOL

Richard Chaffers died in 1765 at the age of only 43. His son William Chaffers was too young to look after the business at Shaws Brow Pottery in Liverpool at that time and so it was taken over by his partner Philip Christian and his son also called Phillip. Christian was discovering that his original Licence was not producing enough soapstone for his soft paste porcelain requirements and so he took out a 14 year Licence including Penruddock, which is situated on the northern side of the track road 400 yds (390m) west of Caunce Head Guest House and about 420 yds (380m) from Mullion Cliffs. The Licence came from the Grylls family from Helston and the Lease rent was 5 guineas per year and the dues were one guinea per ton. By the 1770s William Chaffers was acting for Philip Christian and Company. In 1773 he obtained a Licence for a completely new deposit at Trethevas in Landwednack Parish, a mile north of Lizard Town from the then landowner Thomas Fonnereau of Bochym. Trethevas has not delivered any obvious signs of being quarried for soapstone and although there are a number of stone quarries on the land, many have been filled up over the years. There were a number of Licence changes during this period. Much of Christians porcelain was exported to the West Indies and America.

The Shaws Brow pottery in Liverpool closed down in 1776.

JOHN THORNELOE - WORCESTER

In 1760 John Thorneloe, a Quaker who had been with Worcester from its inception came to Cornwall to supervise a new quarry on behalf of the Worcester partners. In order to complete the process he reportedly stayed as a guest for several weeks at the house of Renatus Kempthorne, a family which had been Mullion residents since the 16th Century.

The quarry, leased from Viscount Falmouth, was in the tenement known as Daroose, east of Teneriffe Farm. When he returned to Worcester Thorneloe took away with him 3 boxes of clay, from which it is said that 3 sets of china were manufactured. One of these sets was given to Mr Kempthorne for his hospitality towards him. The current location of these 3 sets is unknown, however some collectors of Worcester Porcelain have acquired pieces over the years. It was initially thought that Daroose was only a narrow vein expected to yield 8-10 tons of soapstone per annum, but this soon developed into a much larger deposit when it was excavated.

Although the licence was for 10 years it was an important site and supplied Worcester for more than 30 yrs. There was no lease rent paid on this licence but the Lords dues were 20 shillings per ton. Worcester worked the quarry at Daroose from 1760 until 1770, when the licence was renewed and a new 21 year licence taken out until 1791. Daroose was certainly a very large and productive soapstone quarry for Worcester and one which unfortunately today cannot be accessed as it lies within the confines of Predannack airfield.

Some of the old routes of the 18th century lanes in the Predannack Woollas are still visible as footpaths but the edges of the site are fenced and the land overgrown with gorse. Access to Daroose Quarry was gained via a lane which now runs south east of Teneriffe Farm. One hundred yards past Teneriffe Farm is the wooden gated lane, adjacent to the boundary between Predannack Wartha and Woollas. The lane leads to the old Daroose Quarry and it was likely that it was one of the routes used to take away soapstone by horse and cart. One hundred and thirty yards (120m) along this overgrown track, on the left hand side is a small overgrown, wooded location, situated behind the Teneriffe Camping & Caravan Site.

On the Tithe Map for Mullion this location is identified as Well Foss Field (Ref 474) and it is believed to be the site of the old

Wheal Foss, no doubt a small soapstone quarry, and part of the area covered by the Worcester Licence. On the 1888 Ordnance Survey Map the mine site is marked as a "disused China Clay Mine". As there are no reports of China Clay in the immediate area this is no doubt an error. All the land is now owned by National Trust. What therefore existed was a line of quarries starting with Mullion Cliff, Penruddock, Wheal Foss and finally Daroose.

BADDELEY AND YATES OF SHROPSHIRE

In January 1760, two Staffordshire Potters John Baddeley of Shelton and William Yates of Newcastle under Lyne jointly took over the Caerthillian Croft setts vacated by Crisp and Sanders. It was a ten year Licence granted by Viscount Falmouth. The lease rent was 12 guineas a year and the Lords dues a guinea a ton. There was a minimum annual production requirement of 12 tons (12.2 metric tons).

The licence was issued on 1st January 1760 by Lord Falmouth to Baddeley and Yates for a term of 10 yrs granting *"Free Liberty, Licence power and authority to dig work and mine in and upon certain veins and loads of mineral earth commonly called Soapy Rock in this land of this ?Lord Falmouth situate, lying and being in the Commons belonging to part of the tenement of Lizzard within the Parish of Landwednack in the County of Cornwall that is to say …"*.(30)

Baddeley was a manufacturer of salt glazed and lead glazed stoneware but from 1755 until 1761 he was a partner in the firm of William Reid and Co of Liverpool which made Lund style porcelain. It is possible that they did not make soaprock porcelain in the Lund manner but did in fact use it to improve the thermal resistivity of their stonewares and earthenwares.

John Baddeley was the brother of Ralph, and the family potted in the Staffordshire town of Shelton for 50 years. (spode ceramics.com) No other potters in Staffordshire are known to have used soaprock and no figures for the amounts used are recorded.

In 1770 the original Worcester Lease at Gew Graze expired, and was put up for sale. An advert appeared in the Sherborne Mercury of 15th October 1770 as follows; *"To be let; all that large well known rich load of porcelaine clay called Gew Grease Soapy Rock in Mullion from which all the rich Worcester china or porcelaine hath hithertoo been made."*

The lease was purchased by John Nancarrow of Breage and Josiah Holdship of Worcester. With the assistance of a local man, Renatus Kempthorne, a Mullion Yeoman, the Worcester Porcelain Company obtained a new Licence at Daroose, on the margins of the Predannack Downs.

The details of the Licence are as follows; *"On 1st January 1770 by and from George Hunt of Lanhydrock in the County of Cornwall to the said John Wall, William Davis, Benjamin Blayney, and Renatus Kempthorn in the Parish of Mullion... licence and authority to dig... veins and loads.... called the Soapyrock in Predannack Common in the Parish of Mullion … beginning from the work then wrought by Gavrigan Tippitt and going on by the bounds that divide the manor of Predannack Wartha from the manor of Predannack Wallas to the corner of Croft Sooth in the possession of John Harry from thence by the road to Erland Pool and from thence by the head to the gate that enters into Predannack Village and the Mineral earth and soapyrock there found in Breakland way (weigh) and carry off … for the term of 21 years... from the day of the date of this lease at the yearly rent of £10 and 10 shillings (10 guineas)and in case in raising a larger quantity than 10 tuns … of soapyrock in any one year, then subject to the payment of one pound and one shilling more for each tun exceeding 10 tuns …"* (Source: Worcester Record Office)

Most of the boundaries of this Licence can be traced and by referring to the 1841 Tithe Map it can be seen that a number of the locations recorded here have now vanished, some lying under the site of the Predannack airfield. The southern edge is the boundary between Predannack Wartha and Woollas, and the Eastern boundary adjoined the Common and was bounded by Erland Pool. This lake does not now exist and one has to return to the Tithe Map in order to locate it where it appears as a large pool or lake called Herlam Pool on the edge of fields known as Great Herlam Croft, Little Herlam Pool Croft and Higher Herlam

Croft. These fields in 1841 were listed as leased by John Harry and although this is the same name on the Licence it is some 70 years after it was issued which highlights the fact that it was common practice in the area for centuries to hand down the christian name of the father to his son.(52)

There is little doubt that the knowledge of the discovery of Soapstone in large quantities at Penruddock and Daroose increased the search in land adjacent to the boundaries created by the Daroose Licence. The adjacent land is in the area of Predannack Woollas stretching in the direction of Kynance and it is no surprise that the Licences which followed incorporated the area of Predannack Woollas, except that no quarries have been found due to the world war two airfield being constructed.

The 1841 Tithe Map records field names on the Home Kynance tenement one mile to the south east of Teneriffe Farm tenement, such as Great and Little Wheal Venture which might be indicative of previously uninvestigated quarries or mines now not visible on the surface. The land in between is now Ministry of Defence owned and not available to access.

Richard Chaffers foreman of works was Gavregan Teppitt, who after working for many years as an "agent" or "manager" remained in Mullion to see out his retirement while his daughter married the local vicar at the time the Rev. Tonken. He died in 1785 at the age of 70 and was buried in the Churchyard at Mullion.

Hannibal Chaffers and a co-executor Phillip Christian continued to produce quality porcelain for a number of years. The deposit at Daroose had been leased for 10 years on behalf of Worcester and during this time had changed ownership being sold by Viscount Falmouth to John Hunt of Lanhydrock. At the same time Hunt granted a new 21 year lease to Holdship on setts on Lizard Common, inland from Caerthillian Croft . The minimum production was 8 tons per annum. Caerthillian Crofts, like Daroose had changed hands being now owned by Sir Christopher Hawkins of Trewithen. Hawkins granted a ten year lease to Josiah Holdship on behalf of the Worcester partners.

There had been an agreement that Holdship would supply the Worcester partners with all their soapstone requirements, as his brother Richard had done before him, until his bankruptcy. Hawkins increased the lease rent to £45 per annum, with lords dues of a guinea a ton and a minimum production of 20 tons. The Worcester partners were not impressed by the increase but needed the soapstone. Sometime in 1772 Philip Christian renewed the earlier Chaffers licence on deposits at Mullion Cliff originally obtained from the Vyvyans of Trelowarren.

A record of sale , published in "A century of potting in the city of Worcester" by Richard Binns records, *"And whereas by indenture bearing date May 4th1776, made between philip Christian the elder, and Philip Christian the younger,both of Liverpool, china manufacturers of the one part, and the said John Wall the elder, Thomas Vernon, William davis the elder, William Davis the younger, and Catherine Cook , of the other part, reciting that by indenture of lease bearing date July 21st 1772, and made between Thomas Vyvyan the elder and Thomas Vyvyan the younger, of Trewan, in the County of Cornwall, Hugh Lyne of the Parish of Mawgan Meanage,of the said county, Oliver Oliver of Poltishaw Parish of Crade, John Nicholas and Thomas Roskilly of Mullion, in the said county, it was witnessed that for a consideration therein named, liberty to work the soapy rock at Predenick Woollas, parish of Mullion, paying to the said Christian, £500 for their interest in the mine or estate of soapyrock for the remainder of the term of 21 years."*(38)

For many years, this Licence was apparently incorrectly interpreted as the one sold by the Christians to Worcester, but it is not correct, as Sonia Parkinson showed and in fact it relates to Predannack Woollas, not Predannack Wartha. This shows the complexity of the Licences and the problems created by not having available accurate and thorough information.(54a)

In 1773 Richard Holdships 21yr Worcester lease of Gew Graze expired and Josiah Holdship and John Nancarrow applied for a further lease. John Nancarrow, a Quaker, was born in St Agnes and was a friend of William Cookworthy. He was an experienced tin miner who had been a mine captain at the Great Work Tin Mine on Tregonning Hill. He had supervised the production of China Clay at Tregonning Hill until 1772 when the Cookworthy Plymouth factory closed and moved to Bristol. With his mining experience he was able to locate fresh deposits of Soaprock although not in the quantities previously mined as this licence was only for 7yrs with a lease rent of £21 a ton and lords dues of a guinea a ton and a minimum annual production of 20 tons. Production was so low that they decided to relinquish the Gew Graze lease and concentrated on the mines at Daroose, Caerthillian Crofts,Lizard Common(40 tons/year) and Mullion Cliff (10 tons/year) which together produced for Worcester 50 tons per year.

By 1773 the Soaprock was in great demand and supply from the mines was not fully able to meet the demand from the Shaws Brow Liverpool factory and as a result William Chaffers, acting on behalf of Phillip Christian and Co. obtained a lease at a new location of Trethewas in Landwednack Parish from Thomas Fonnereau of Bochym. Trethvas as it is now called is one mile north of Lizard Village and stretches east to the coast. In July the same year he renewed the lease at Penruddock for a further 7 years until 1780 on behalf of Christian. In 1775 Christian gave up the Liverpool pottery and the leases were sold to Worcester. On 8th June 1775, the Staffordshire potter Josiah Wedgwood (1730-1795), who had had his right leg amputated in 1768, went on a tour of the county looking for new clay deposits along with John Turner. He visited the soaprock workings at Gew Graze and was not impressed. He described how *"The way down to the rock was so very steep and bad and the sea roaring at the bottom , that none of us durst venture down it,except our guide, who ran down like a goat, and after being some time out of sight returned and brought us up some of the soaprock in his pocket handkerchief."* The following day he met Lord Falmouths agent at Tregothnan who informed him that *"the Worcester Company had a lease of the sett for 10 guineas a year and a guinea per ton for all they raised above 10 tons per annum. But they never having paid any rent, their lease is forfeited and we may have a lease of the same if we choose it."*(54) Wedgwood chose not to use the soapstone but subsequently to the sale of the Worcester company in 1783 it was acquired by Flight and Barr. It was said however that the nature of the veins and the heavy expenses of blasting the rock made it an unprofitable speculation.(54)

There is no record of Wedgwood ever using soaprock on a commercial basis but he did use the Transfer Printing method introduced by the Worcester Porcelain Company in the 1750s.Wedgwood instead was a major producer of Earthenware, his creamware having Royal patronage, as well as being exported all over the world. It is worth pointing out that research of the original record of the journey in 1775 made by Wedgwood in his "Commonplace book"conducted by Sonia Parkinson indicates that he may actually have recorded a visit to Kynance Cove, not Gew Graze. Wedgwood wrote "Guinans Cove" crossed out the "Gui" and replaced it with "Ky". In addition he recorded that the party travelled not the 2 miles from Lizard village which would have taken them to Gew Graze, but 1 and 1/2 miles which would have taken them to Kynance.(54a)

There is always danger involved in mining and quarrying operations and it is important to note that working at Gew Graze may not have been without its risks. Again, I have to say that this cannot be backed up by currently available documentary evidence, but

2 pieces of Caughley ware c1790
Pieces donated by Peter Starling, Caughley Soc.

Caughley 'Conversation'
mask-headed jug c1785
Photo donated by Peter Starling, Caughley Soc.

it relates to a story passed down and sourced from 3 people, that there was an incident at one of the Gew Graze quarries caused by the collapse of part of the cliff or a rock arch which resulted in the deaths of several miners. The story goes on to say that the bodies of the miners were buried close to Gew Graze in unmarked graves.

POTTERS SOAPROCK COMPANY OF MULLION

According to the research of John Penderill-Church, in 1770 Thomas Trounson, a local Mullion man, leased a brand new soaprock deposit at Meaver Vean, the most Northerly of the Lizard soaprock deposits. It is believed that he was only able to supply between 7-10 tons per year but could only work the deposit in the summer months. In 1777 he was approached by John Nicholas of Cury with a suggestion that a proper company be formed to supply soaprock on a larger scale. A fourth partner was found , John Lean of Redruth , described as a tinner, but apparently with shipping connections, and so the Potters Soaprock Company was formed. There is no surviving record of the original Lease but it was apparently referred to by the Hon Frances Boscawen in the renewal granted to the Potters Soaprock Company in 1777. On 25th March 1777 a Licence was granted by Frances Boscawen to John Nicholas of Cury, John Lean of Redruth, Tinner, William Thomas and Thomas Trounson both of Mullion, Yeomen, for 7 years, to mine all that clay earth or soft rock commonly called soapy rock clay in Meaver, alias Meaver Vean in Mullion now in the possession of Thomas Trounson, for dues of 21 shillings (1 Guinea) a ton. It was agreed between Hon Frances Boscawens agent and the partners that they should produce as much as the deposit would yield, in their own interests as much as Boscawen and this amount was 7-14 tons per annum. By the end of the lease the deposit was likely worked out and it was not renewed. The area was visited by Penderill-Church in the 1970s who believed it to be *a long ovoid site close to the Mullion- Penhale road*.(30)(5a)

Consideration has to be given to the fact that the course of the road in 1841 may not have been the road in 1770 because an older lane or road existed from Meaver to Penhale which took a route through land at Meaver Crease. This was partly closed by 1841.

There are a number of old quarries in this locality including a large roadside quarry, which does lie on Serpentine bedrock and was recently built upon. The same applies to a smaller water filled quarry a short distance away on Trednow land, also lying on the same outcrop of serpentine. Although the water has now dried up at this site, and it has been filled with rubbish over the years, an escarpment is visible surrounding this quarry which is approximately 12-15 foot in height, giving it a similar appearance to Penruddock. The existence of a water filled quarry may support the original information about work at the Meaver site only being possible in the summer months.

A large quarry close to Meaver Crease which has been filled in during the last 100 years, lies on the course of the older Meaver to Penhale road. In addition there are two water filled clay pits on the north side of the current road where the serpentine resumes, about 250 yards (228 metres) from the Penhale junction, which was listed as two clay pits in the 1841 Tithe Map (Ref 911) so identification of this quarry is complex and there may have been more than one source. The 1841 Tithe Map apportionments indicates a field on the land of Trednow opposite the site of the clay pit (Ref 911) named "White Rock Field" (Ref 951) - possibly a reference to soaprock. Small quarries would extract any available stone for which there was a massive requirement in the area for roads, cornish hedges and walls, and building of houses.

THOMAS TURNER AND AMBROSE GALLIMORE OF CAUGHLEY

In 1750 an earthenware pottery was started by Edward Browne at Caughley in Shropshire on the banks of the River Severn and in 1754 a 62 year lease was taken by the Quaker Ambrose Gallimore, who had his origins in the Staffordshire potteries. In 1772 he was joined by Thomas Turner, who had trained as an artist and potter under Robert Hancock at Worcester and who was familiar with the soaprock process. The Pottery, the two and three storey Salopian China Manufactory, was built and adapted to incorporate the use of soapstone in the formula which appears to have been completed about 1775. Turner had been an associate of William Davis, Richard Holdship, John Thorneloe and others and knew about the steatitic porcelain process. By

1775 he was joined by Robert Hancock, the engraver and decorator, who had moved on from Worcester. There is no evidence of a Soapstone Licence but it is possible that they obtained soapstone from Trounson, as this appears to be the only available source at this time. The soapstone would need to be crushed to a fine powder prior to use and there were grinding mills near to the porcelain works at Calcutts near Broseley and at the Smithies near Willey which may have been used. There was also a source of coal,and many tons of coal were used in the firing processes.(56) In 1776 Turner visited the Lizard to obtain a working soapstone licence and met Gavregan Teppit, now unemployed after the transfer to Worcester of the Mullion Cliff and Penruddock Quarries of Chaffers and Christian. Attention was turned again to the abandoned Gew Graze workings and eventually viable soapstone was located. The Worcester Licence did not expire until 1780. Turner and Gallimore were granted a special licence covering the period from October 1776 until the official expiry in 1780 and then a 14 year licence to work from 1780 until 1794. The first part Licence from Lord Falmouth was a £100 buy out, with £21 Lease rent and a guinea a ton Lords dues and the 14 year Licence also £21 lease rent per annum and and a minimum production of 20 tons (20.3 metric tons) per annum, with Lords dues of a guinea for each ton over 20 tons.

Apparently Turner celebrated the new 14 year licence by bringing out a Willow Pattern service in Porcelain, subsequently much copied in earthenware.(57)

In 1778 Turner obtained a 14 year licence from Thomas Grylls and Peter Prisk at Predannack Downs, which was to operate at Penruddock until 1792.

In 1781 the Worcester lease of Caerthillian Crofts now owned by Sir Christopher Hawkins (Kynance, Pentreath and Caerthillian Mill) was up for renewal. Hawkins wanted £66 lease rent per annum for setts which according to Penderill-Churchs research of the Johnstone papers in Truro record office came from *"A cove or sand beach called by the name of Kynance and Cathillian Hill in Lizard."*

On the 29th September 1792 Turner obtained a licence from Thomas Grylls and Peter Priske to quarry or mine for soapstone throughout the area of Predannack Woollas, downs or commons formerly worked by Philip Christian senior and junior.

THOMAS FLIGHT AND ROBERT CHAMBERLAIN OF WORCESTER

A renewed licence was taken out but two years later in 1783 Josiah Holdship and William Davis senior, the last two surviving founding members of the Worcester company died ending the Quaker involvement after 32 years. The Worcester factory was bought by the London agent Thomas Flight of Hockney in Middlesex for £3000 for his two sons John Flight (1766-1791),and Joseph Flight (1762-1838). He took over the company and the Soaprock Licences which had been taken out by Holdship on behalf of the company. The Worcester Company continued to attract some of the finest porcelain artists in the Country and ran a 7 year apprenticeship scheme for young people, producing fine decorators. John Flight was to make a visit to France where he studied the latest French designs. In 1783 after Thomas Flight bought the factory some technical difficulties had arisen aggravated by the fact that their main decorator Robert Chamberlain left and set up a rival factory in Severn Street Worcester. Chamberlain was believed to have been the first apprentice in the Doctor John Wall era.

Chamberlain became very successful. He was supplied with undecorated porcelain by Thomas Turner, made at his Caughley works, while Chamberlain decorated both for Turner and themselves. From the late 1780s there were visits made to the Worcester establishment by King George III and Queen Charlotte. They made regular visits to the Worcester Music Meeting, the forerunner of the three choirs festival, and paid the factory a visit. They were impressed by the quality of porcelain produced and made orders totalling many hundreds of pounds and after a visit in 1788 issued Worcester with their first Royal warrant in 1789, allowing Flight to use the Royal Coat of Arms and the words "Manufacturers to their Majesties". As a result there were visits and orders from Royalty and nobility alike and these orders spread and a new London shop at Number 1 Coventry Street off Piccadilly Circus was opened.

JOSEPH FLIGHT/MARTIN BARR OF WORCESTER

John Flight died in 1791 at just 25 years of age, and Joseph Flight and took Martin Barr into partnership.

In 1791 Thomas Flight came down to Cornwall on an expedition to search for new sources of Soaprock. He wanted to make sure that the Worcester company had adequate soaprock for their operation. The Mullion Cliff Licence taken out in 1775 was due to expire in 1791 and the Penruddock Licence expired in 1780. Daroose and Caerthillian were also due to expire. The Caerthillian setts had changed hands to William Crowgey of Penryn and Daroose setts were owned by George Hunt of Lanhydrock. During June he negotiated a new lease for the Caerthillian setts as well as negotiating with 3 landowners for the lease of setts on the Lizard Common. Some setts had been previously leased but there were new ones. The agreements were drawn up between Thomas Flight of Hockney in Middlesex and the Hunt family at Lanhydrock, also between Flight and William Crowgey of Penryn (Caerthillian and Lizard Common), George Hunt of Westminster (Daroose) and Thomas Fonnereau of Bochym (Trethevas). Each of the 3 leases took effect on Midsummers Day June 24th 1791 and were for terms of 21 yrs up to 1812, with no lease rent, lords dues of 20 shillings/ton and a minimum of 8 tons produced annually per landowner, making 24 tons in all per annum.

Thomas Flight also instigated a further search at Gew Graze where a new seam inland from the original quarries was located for which a proving licence was obtained until 1794.(5a) A full Lease was obtained but the seams did not yield as much as expected and production was subsequently reduced from 20 tons (20.3 metric tons) to 8-10 tons per year. Flight also took over the lease at Daroose which had 10 yrs to run up to 1801.

THOMAS TURNER AND ANDREW GALLIMORE OF CAUGHLEY

In 1792 Thomas Turner turned his attention again to the Predannack setts. Originally thought of as being at Penruddock and Mullion Cliff, it now seems that they may be alternatively located in the Predannack Woollas at, if Sonia Parkinson is correct, a currently unidentified location.(30b) They took out a 14yr lease which was due to expire in 1806 with Andrew Gallimore, the son of his earlier partner Ambrose Gallimore. The lease rent was 5 guineas per annum and with Lords dues of a Guinea a ton from Thomas Grylls and Peter Prisk. Thomas Turner did not remain at Caughley to see out this lease and in 1799 sold out to John Rose and Edward Blakeways who were running the Coalport factory. They were to continue to use soapstone in small amounts in their products.

A copy of the Indenture issued to Thomas Turner, covers all the land previously worked by Philip Christian and son, and includes land in Predannack Woollas. The work allowed to be conducted in this Licence is interesting because it talks at length about the authority to dig,work,mine,search for and raise clay, otherwise soapy rock as well as other minerals and especially the sinking of shaft,shafts,or pits, the driving of adits, or Drifts. It further allows the building of an engine, engines, shed or sheds, or other buildings or conveniences, previously unheard of on this part of the Lizard. The Indenture also describes the use of ropes,buckets, engines and other materials, Kebbles (Large buckets), windlists (Windlass) or tackle and ensures that all adits are kept open, sufficiently inspected, repaired and kept in good order, the bottoms of any adits are cleared of "deads" and all hedges and fences surrounding adits are kept repaired. This implies a right to the use of underground working to obtain the soapstone.(58)

JOSEPH FLIGHT, MARTIN BARR & MARTIN BARR JNR OF WORCESTER

In 1794 Joseph Flight and Martin Barr (1757-1813) took over the Gew Graze lease granted by George Boscawen, Viscount Falmouth.They paid £52-10 shillings for the 14 year Lease, a lease rent of a guinea a ton and dues of a guinea a ton for all soaprock in excess of 20 tons, the minimum permitted production.

The Worcester partnership worked it for its full term. The new setts were described as lying "from a rock on the Carn, on the east of the old working of Gew Graze mine, to the east, to a stone fixed between the said Rock and the corner of the hedge to the south of the said Carn , and from thence in a straight line to a Rock on the Carn to the north of the said Cellar and from that Rock and also from that rock to the east, one hundred fathoms north north east."(5a)

The exact location is not certain but may be along the valley leading up from Gew Graze. The setts consisted of a roughly rectangular area inland from the old quarry and extending for 600 feet. After expiry of this Licence Flight and Barr continued to take soapstone from their other deposits at Mullion, Caerthillian, Daroose, Trethevas and Lizard Common, until they became exhausted. In 1804 Martin Barr Junior (1784-1848) joined the Worcester partnership and in the next 10 years some of the finest porcelain ever made was produced at Warmstry House. Porcelain services were made to customers requests and during this time the quality of the painters, such as William Billingsley and John Pennington, produced outstanding work on such scenes as landscapes,castles and country houses. Botanical work became popular with rare specimens painted on porcelain. In the 18th and 19th centuries Chinese Porcelain decorated with coats of arms was a huge status symbol but the sets sometimes took years to be produced by the Chinese and there were often mistakes made by the Chinese artists who did not understand their instructions and Worcester produced a better more reliable alternative. Customers included the Prince of Wales,Tzar Alexander I, The Duke of York, King George III, King William IV, The Duke of Clarence, the Imam of Muscat, and the Marquis of Buckingham. The Prince of Wales, for example, spent huge amounts on the Brighton Pavilion and in 1807 spent thousands of pounds on Imari style dinner services from Barr, Flight and Barr.(38)

It has been speculated that Mullion was used as the reception centre for all soapstone produced on Predannack Downs,Caerthillian and Lizard Common, the stone being taken by cart or by boat to Mullion Cove where the old pilchard cellars had been converted to take soapstone. Some of the Flight Licences of 1791 had been renewed in 1812 when they ended their term, but Caerthillian and Lizard Common did not finish their final terms as they were becoming exhausted.

JOSEPH FLIGHT OF WORCESTER

In 1813 Martin Barr died, and Joseph Flight became the principal shareholder, with George and Martin Barr as juniors. The company continued, but the demand for rich classical porcelain gradually diminished, with the new industrialists preferring a different style, and the success was never quite the same. The Flight Licences were renewed in 1812 but although production at Worcester was beginning to slow down the industry continued to use soaprock.

LIST OF PROPRIETORS OF THE WORCESTER PORCELAIN WORKS 1751-1840

1751-1772 John Wall (MD) David Henry Rev. Thomas Vernon Richard Holdship, William Davis Mary Blayney, Rev. Benjamin Blayney, William Oliver Richard Cook, Samuel Bradley, John Salway Henry Cook, Rev.Samuel Pritchett, Germain Lavie, John Thorneloe.
1772-1774 John Wall the elder (MD), William Davis the elder, an apothecary William Davis the younger Rev. Thomas Vernon Robert Hancock the engraver Richard Cook of London.
1774-1776 John Wall the elder (MD), William Davis, the elder Rev. Thomas Vernon, William Davis the younger Richard Cook of London.
1776-1783 William Davis the elder, William Davis the younger Rev. Thomas Vernon. 1783-1792 Joseph Flight John Flight.
1793-1807 Joseph Flight Martin Barr
1807-1813 Martin Barr Joseph Flight Martin Barr junior.
1813-1829 Joseph Flight Martin Barr George Barr
1829-1840 Martin Barr George Barr
1840 Chamberlain, Flight and Barr merge to form one company.(60)

The Worcester Factory were by far the largest users of Soapstone on the west coast of the Lizard. They begun quarrying in 1752 at Gew Graze, with the Licence taken over from Benjamin Lund and subsequently extended this until1790. In 1760 they also extended to Daroose with a 21 year lease and further bought into Caerthillian, one of the sites close to Mullion Cove and Lizard Downs. They were also one of the last potteries to leave the area having licences until the 1820s at Gew Graze. It has been suggested that they may have been trying to buy up all the soapstone in the area and create a monopoly of production but this did not occur and unlike Cookworthy and Champion with their China Clay, they never patented their soapstone porcelain.

By the early 19th century China Clay was beginning to supersede soapstone, just as bone china had taken the place of other types of soft paste porcelain. According to local records the last shipment of soapstone sent to Worcester was in 1822. (5a) The death of Flight in 1829 was at a time of depression within the trade and adversely affected the Company. It should be remembered that these rich highly decorated wares were not the only ones produced. Flight and Chamberlain also produced more general wares,often to rival the earthenware produced by Staffordshire. From 1830 the Staffordshire potters made huge progress in the manufacture of porcelain, they improved the quality of their earthenware and introduced their "iron-stone china", a porcelain substitute which could be mass produced. It was introduced and patented by William Turner at Longton in Stafforshire in 1800 and then the patent was sold to Josiah Spode in 1805.

There was continual experimentation with different combinations of materials to try and improve the porcelain formula and the methods of production, for hundreds of thousands of pieces were produced. Barr, Flight and Barr continued to produce the old classical porcelain designs with alternatives to the soapstone, and by 1840 they had merged with their old rival Chamberlain and between them continued to produce fine porcelain through the Victorian era ... but but by this time, not with soapstone.

In 1851 the Severn Street Factory expanded from 70 to 700 employees, concentrating on figurines and vases and in 1862 Royal Worcester was formed. The company continued to produce porcelain products, including industrial products for the Government, for the next 88 years before becoming a Public Company in 1954. In 2001 Queen Elizabeth and the Duke of Edinburgh visited Worcester as part of the 250th Anniversary Celebrations and in 2006 Ceramic Production finally finished at Severn Street, leaving only the top painting and Gilding operations there. The Royal Worcester name was purchased by Portmeirion in 2009 and the Severn Street factory closed.

Detailed information about the day to day activities of the quarries even in the 19th century is hard to find but in 1808 at Gew Graze 500lb of soaprock was being raised each week on behalf of Flight and Barr at Worcester by 5 local miners. The soaprock was sorted and graded by 3 women who packed it into casks for shipment to Worcester. In 1808 the Rev. Richard Warner of Bath, on a visit to Cornwall wrote; *"The village of Mullion detected from afar by the lofty tower of its church is reached without difficulty …….. but to discover the way beyond this place, hoc opus, hie labor est. Indeed had we not known that the steatite or soap rock quarries lay immediately on the coast, it would have been beyond ilic reach even of our acuteness to have found them out. Keeping as close to the cliff as it was practical, we at length, descended into a narrow valley where we perceived the object of which we were in search, and the workmen employed in extracting the fossil from the rock. The name steatite has been imposed upon this production from its appearance and texture, for both to the eye and the touch it bears the strongest resemblance to soap… Five men are employed in digging the article, of which they procure about 500lbs per week, and 3 or 4 women in an adjoining building sort the steatite when it is brought to them , separating the finer masses from the grosser, and packing it in barrels for exportation. The former is valued at upwards of 20 shillings per ton, the latter of course sells at a reduced price. Messrs Flight and Barr of Worcester are the owners of the quarry and consume the greatest part of its produce, using it in their china manufactory by mixing about one third of the best steatite with the other porcelain earths, a combination which imparts to the ware a most beautiful china like appearance"*(61)

As late as 1815 an advertisement appeared in the West Briton for April 21st asking for tenders to ship 80 tons of soapstone from Mullion across Mounts Bay to Penzance, for forwarding to Worcester, *"To owners of Vessels Wanted A vessel to remove 80 tons of Soap Rock Clay from the Cove at Mullion across the Bay to Penzance Application to be made to Mr Jethroe Hornblower Whitehall, near Redruth who will contract for the same Whitehall April 19th 1815."* Hornblower had vessels which travelled directly from Penzance to Swansea and Worcester.(5a)

China Clay was rapidly superseding soapstone, just as bone china had taken the place of other types of soft paste porcelain. At this stage it is worth acknowledging the part played by the travelling Victorian clergy in recording and providing information of their travels, particularly so in the case of travels through Cornwall, with the likes of William Borlase, Richard Pococke, Charles Johns, Richard Warner and Edmund Harvey. They were often some of the few learned and literate men of their era, and their observation and contribution has left some of the only literary references available to us today.

LEWIS DILLWYN OF SWANSEA

In 1803 William Weston Young, a Bristol businessman and botanist was in financial difficulties and moved to Swansea where he obtained employment under a fellow Quaker Lewis Weston Dillwyn as a draftsman and Porcelain decorator at his Cambrian Pottery.

The pottery had originally been set up based upon the business ideas of Josiah Wedgwood. Both Young and Dillwyn had a huge interest in natural history reflected in the decoration of the pottery. One of the best Worcester painters of porcelain was a man called William Billingsley. In the early 1800s he had moved from Derby to set up his own small pottery factory but in 1808 moved to Worcester under Flight, Barr and Barr, where he was responsible for making improvements to the porcelain. Under the terms of his employment, he had to sign a contract preventing him from disclosing porcelain recipes to a third party but got around this by making the porcelain himself and in 1813 went on to Nantgarw in Glamorgan where, along with his son in law William Walker he set up his own porcelain factory, where they received financial backing from the Quaker businessman William Weston Young. The South Wales porcelain pottery industry was just beginning to develop but Billingsley in his attempts to produce his Worcester style porcelain had got the formula wrong and most of the products failed in the firing. In 1814 Dillwyn provided them with his own advice and with the introduction of a new kiln and financial backing offered them the chance to use the Cambrian factory. At the end of 1814 new trials started and production resumed. The quality of the porcelain and the decoration received acclaim but there were still serious problems with the firing. They subsequently left the Cambrian Pottery and moved to Coalport.(65)

On December 2nd 1814 the very last west coast soapstone lease had been taken out by Lewis Weston Dillwyn. Dillwyn obtained a seven year lease at Gew Graze from Viscount Falmouth, effective from September 29th, though not valid until December. The lease rent was £75 per annum with a minimum production of 15 tons per annum and the Lords dues of £5 per ton for all soapstone raised in excess of 15 tons. At the same time Dillwyn was also taking supplies of china clay from St Austell, and in 1817 he handed over control to Thomas and John Bevington where there was change in production to produce the new glazed earthenware.

By 1822 it appears that they no longer took soapstone from their lease. One of the people with a wide knowledge of South Wales Pottery was in fact E.E. Morton-Nance, mentioned several times in this book for his research into the Soapstone Licences. He was born in Cardiff in 1873 of Cornish Parents before retiring to St.Ives. In 1895 he

Photo of diagram of the quarry sites showing serpentine boundaries.

Caughley 'Fisherman' mask-headed jug c1785

taught at Swansea Grammar School and while there began collecting the South Wales pottery and porcelain and later writing a specialist book on the subject which was published in 1942. He formed one of the largest collections of South Wales and Nantgarw pottery and porcelain ever made, now in the National Museum of Wales. He also assisted in the foundation of the Federation of Old Cornwall Societies,which first took place in 1920 and was one of the founder members of the Cornish Gorsedd.

Within the opening years of the 19th century searches were made for new deposits of soapstone, while older ones were beginning to be reworked.

On 14th August 1810 William Jenkins wrote *" There seems to be an increased enquiry lately after the soapyrock. John Williams of Scorrier House,(Tin Miner from Redruth) applied a few days back for a grant of one spot where there are now the marks of some old workings for that article in Predannack, near the village. William Bennets of Camborne hath since applied for another spot not far from the Cove (Mullion). It is a vein of soapy nature discovered in the old adit, I think,"* He adds *"the company who are now, and have been for years back, digging this article out of Predannack Woollas pay about 20 shillings or 21 shillings per ton for Lords dues. In the same month an application was received from the adventurers in South Wheal Unity for the rising and manufacture of any soapyrock or clay which they may have discovered in clearing or driving the present adit belonging to that unfortunate concern."*(64) This indicates that it was not only the main pottery companies who were looking to obtain soapstone, although they could have been agents acting on behalf of the porcelain companies including Worcester.

There were also small deposits of Soapstone on the eastern side of the Lizard. One pure white vein at Black Head was described by Johns in 1848 as being kept secret but provided material for brooches and letter weights, confirming the existence of at least one localised cottage industry.(65)

Although there may be other Licences not yet traced, the last apparent Licence which mentions soaprock was issued in 1853 but was on the eastern side of the Lizard and in conjunction with the working of serpentine. Evelyn, Viscount Falmouth issued a Licence to Thomas Jackson of Commercial Road Pimlico for Serpentine stone, Steatite stone,Soapstone, Diallage, and other stone of similar kind at Halwoon, or Pisgah, and Carne, Mount Batt and Gwendreath in the Parish of Grade. This term was for 21 years from 1st November 1853. The minimum rent was £50 per ton and dues 4 shillings (20 pence) per ton.

The lateness of this Licence and the incorporation of a number of minerals may be connected with the commercial carving of Serpentine and other materials which still takes place in and near Lizard Village. It was possibly the distance from the other raw materials, or the lack of suitable lines of transport or suitability of the markets, which prevented porcelain making taking place in Cornwall. The constituents, whether it be fuel for the kilns, availability of trained or skilled decorators, or clay for the pots came from all parts of the country, and reserves had to be sufficient to sustain the factories.

Small hand turned steatite vase

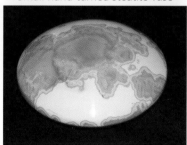

Small hand turned steatite paperweight

The developing markets at the start of the Industrial Revolution were not just in England but in America, Europe and elsewhere. There is still a small serpentine turning industry on the "Soaprock Coast", but today there is only one small producer of Porcelain, which is in Lizard village, so perhaps some of those early pieces might one day be replicated. What is known is that the last known West Coast Licence expired in 1828.

In 1840 B.P. Smith in his book " A trip to the Far West" wrote that in the early 19th Century the supply of soaprock was diminishing but as late as 1840 carts were still described as coming from the Lizard with a white clay or mineral used for china in Swansea,Liverpool and Staffordshire Potteries, to St. Michaels Mount, from where it seems to have been shipped in barrels. This may have been a modern reference to an earlier use of the soapstone.(62)

In 1848 the Rev. C.A. Johns noted that the industry had practically disappeared, the only use for the mineral then being the manufacture of Epsom salts. Johns, walking the coast north from Kynance reported that *"The Soap Rock is generally considered the great point of attraction in this direction,in their eagerness to visit which tourists frequently neglect the intervening coast, but if they follow the edge of the cliff the whole of the way they will be richly repaid for their trouble."* Passing The Rill, the Horse and Pigeon Hugo he wrote… *" a few steps further on we gain view of the very remarkable cove, Gue Graze, as it is marked in the maps,or as it is called by the people of the neighbourhood, Due Greze,in the ravine leading down to which is the Soap Rock. The soap rock is situated in a deep ravine which runs down to this cove,it was formerly quarried , and large quantities of steatite, or soapstone was carried away and employed in the manufacture of the finer kinds of porcelain. Of late years a material, equally well adapted for the purpose has been obtained from the decomposed feldspar which is found in great abundance near St. Austle, and as this can be procured at a much less expense , the use of soapstone has been discontinued. The only economic purpose to which the minerals of the district are applied is to the manufacture of Epsom salts, for which a cargo is occasionally exported."(45)*

13. William Cookworthy (1705-1780)

It would be inappropriate not to include some information about a well known west country man,William Cookworthy. He was born in 1705 of Quaker parents in Kingsbridge,Devon but his father died when he was 13 yrs old and the family investment in the South Sea Company failed. He reportedly walked to London because he had no money, and there he became an apprentice to two Quaker apothecary brothers called Bevan.

In 1726 Bevan started a pharmacy business in Plymouth and by 1735 Cookworthy was a partner in the business. He became interested in porcelain manufacture through the letters of the French Jesuit priest, working in China, Pere D`Entrocolles, and in 1745 an American businessman tried to interest him in importing clays found in Virginia. He

Soapstone/Serpentine bible front

Soapstone/Serpentine bible spine

Soapstone from Gew Graze with black inclusions.

decided to look locally and was able to locate a material called China Clay, also known as Moorstone or Growan Clay in Cornwall in Breage and at Tregonning Hill in 1746.

John Nancarrow, also a Quaker, who lived at Gunwalloe for a time, had been manager of the Godolphin group of mines and was also a friend of Cookworthy and was also heavily involved with the soapstone working on the Lizard. He was an experienced tin miner and also had also been involved in raising clay from other areas of Cornwall. It is believed that he advised Cookworthy of the location of a kaolin like clay at Tregonning Hill where local workers used to repair small local kilns.

Cookworthy experimented and found that when either petuntse (aluminium and potassium silicate), plus china stone or kaolin (aluminium silicate) and china clay were fired together at high temperatures(1200-1400 degrees Centigrade), both combinations produced porcelain. He took leases on various clay pits on Tregonning Hill, which was exported through Porthleven to Plymouth, where Cookworthy had a small factory. The Tregonning Hill clay contained mica and did not give the required quality for him, but eventually with the discovery and suitability of China Clay (kaolin) in St. Austell he was able to find an investor in Thomas Pitt who owned the land where this better quality kaolin was found. Pitt who later became Lord Camelford also became a partner with Cookworthy, establishing the Plymouth China Works making decorated tea services jugs and vases. It took him until 1768 to file a Patent specification which gave him exclusive use of China Clay and China Stone.

The Plymouth venture proved unprofitable and he amalgamated with a pottery in Bristol making his cousin Richard Champion manager and in 1774 he sold out to him. In 1777 Champion tried to renew the Cookworthy patent but received opposition from Josiah Wedgwood and others. The patent formula was upheld but the use of Kaolin was released so that other potters could make use of it. The high legal costs forced Champion to sell the patent to the New Hall Pottery in Staffordshire. It is sometimes said that Cookworthy was responsible for porcelain manufacture in the South West and indeed he developed some porcelain based on China Clay or Kaolin, but he did not use Soapstone which was in widespread use some 20 years earlier.

The earliest piece of hard paste porcelain attributable to him is a blue decorated mug in the British Museum and is dated at 1768. Eventually with the development of new formulae China Clay and the release to other companies it overtook the use of soaprock in ceramic products and since its discovery over 120 million tons have been produced.(66)

'Pickle dishes' Worcester Museum

Plate and vases Worcester Museum

The Donaldson Collection

14. A cottage industry

There has long been a "cottage industry" on the Lizard, connected to the turning of Serpentine and soapstone objects. The current industry revolves mainly around the turning of Serpentine, and while the turning of Lizard soapstone has taken place it has now almost disappeared. The skill, patience and experience required is enormous. On the Lizard, Soapstone is mainly found as veins rather than soapstone masses, although pockets of workable material still exist.

An elderly Mullion resident and Old Cornwall Society member provided information about an artifact which had been handed down through the family. It was believed that this artifact was connected to the early soaprock mining at Gew Graze, and was made from material sourced in the early days of the quarrying. It has never been away from the family. The artifact was a small stone replica "Bible" made from cut and polished serpentine and soaprock. See the photograph on page 61. It is approximately 4 inches long by 3 inches wide and about an inch in depth. The core of the Bible is made from best quality polished red and green Serpentine and lined with a border of white soaprock with black inclusions. A central section of Serpentine on the front and the back bears a raised rectangular plinth in which a small white soaprock cross, was inlaid. The spine of the "book" is tooled and curved to give the impression of being leather bound, with 4 small soaprock ribs. Although in good condition there is some damage to one of the covers. It is said that it is made with soapstone which had originated from Gew Graze in the early days of the mining and in fact the original family member who possessed this Bible was involved with the earliest working of the soapstone there. In fact investigation has revealed that there are still small quantities of this type of soapstone still in situ there. Further more it would appear that this replica Bible may be almost unique and was possibly part of a local "cottage industry" in existence at this time.

There is an extraordinary amount of skill involved in cutting and shaping such an object which may be almost unique. Over the years many artifacts would have been manufactured but there is evidence that this unique industry still survives today. I was fortunate enough to be able to meet an elderly Lizard resident who still makes a small number of "steatite" artifacts today. The patience and skill involved is extraordinary and begins by finding the right piece of soapstone to work. There are a few small sites left which provide the appropriate material which is subsequently roughly shaped and then turned and polished on a small lathe over many hours. The results can be seen in the photographs of the vase and the paperweight on page 60.

15. Worcester Porcelain Museum

The first Royal Worcester Porcelain Museum was opened in November 1879 thanks to the forethought of Richard William Binns, Managing Director, Company Director and first company historian who bought up examples of early Worcester and other works of Art to inspire his workforce. Following his death a lot of works including Porcelain were sold. Charles William Dyson Perrins, a Director of the Worcester company (whose family created the recipe of Lea & Perrins Worcestershire Sauce), formed a large private collection of 18th century Worcester porcelain and then in 1926 purchased the museum collection and library on the understanding that it would remain on display at the factory in his lifetime. In1934 he purchased the Royal Worcester factory and after the war

Early sauceboat Worcester Museum

Ken Russell Worcester Master Gilder

Gilding

Porcelain production at 'Pentreath Porcelain' on The Lizard today

reunited his own collection with that of the original museum. In 1967 the museum was rehoused in its current location next to the old factory.

In 1995 a special porcelain collection decorated by James Giles was bequeathed by Gerald Coke and the museum was totally refurbished. It is now called the Worcester Porcelain Museum. It is well worth a visit. Many examples of early steatitic porcelain are housed in the museum and contain soapstone which originated in the quarries of the Lizard.

Worcester Porcelain has always maintained high standards of decoration and today at the Museum the quality and artistry can be seen performed by Master Gilder Ken Russell. Ken has been with the company since 1950 and has been involved with all the major designs since that time. He has gilded services of china for H.M.The Queen, U.S. Presidents, Arab Sultans and other Heads of state. Although Retired he can be seen at the museum regularly practicing his skills.

Three dot painter style c1753

Early Worcester teapot 1750's

16. Conclusion

Although a number of potteries such as Vauxhall, Caughley, Liverpool and Swansea sought and obtained the advantages offered by the Lizard Soaprock in the 18th and early 19th Centuries, there is a special link between the Worcester Porcelain Company and the Cornish Soaprock Quarries of the Mullion area of the Lizard Peninsula. From the earliest days of the 18th Century Soaprock was believed to have special properties and these were described by the likes of Dr. Borlase, and Emmanuel Da Costa. Travellers and writers alike came to Gew Graze, recorded their observations and ideas and formed the opinion that soaprock could have a valid use in the manufacture of porcelain. In Mullion Parish the main quarries were at Gew Graze (Soapy Cove), Kynance, Daroose, Penruddock,Mullion Cliff and at Meaver Vean, whilst in Landwednack Parish they were at Caerthillian, Pentreath, Trethevas and the Lizard Downs. Many smaller soapstone quarries or pits were likely to have existed, since being used for stone or infilled with rubbish.

It has now been established that the extent of the quarrying at Mullion Cove has far exceeded that which was previously known, and included the whole area from Henscath right around to The Vro. It included not only quarrying but also hard rock mining and provided hundreds of tons of soapstone for the porcelain industry. There is no doubt that Mullion Cove, as well as being a site of outstanding natural beauty has an Industrial Heritage which has almost been forgotten. The marks of that Heritage are still visible, and anyone standing on the Harbour Wall today is lucky enough to still be able to see the panorama where it all unfolded over 250 years ago.

Furthermore and importantly the ancient quay at Pengersick has been identified, from which the Gew Graze soapstone was transported.

The early experiments by Benjamin Lund with crushed Soaprock from Gew Graze were successful enough to produce the first quality porcelain but it was not until newly formed Worcester Porcelain Company with their new business ideas took over Lunds pottery in Bristol and his Soaprock Mining Licence on the Lizard that production in Britain began to expand, skilfully creating products which proved to be competitive to the imported Chinese Porcelain. By 1789 they were awarded a Royal Warrant by King George III and later two further Royal Warrants, in 1807 by the Prince of Wales and in 1808 by the Princess of Wales and up until 2009 was still in Service to the Crown by Appointment to Queen Elizabeth II. Royal Worcester traded until June 14th 2009 when it was taken over by Portmeirion after 258 years producing millions of items for the British and World markets. It has some of the most admired products and collected products in the world.

Other porcelain potteries such as that of Crisp and Sanders at Vauxhall in London, Chaffers and Podmore at Shaws Brow in Liverpool, Turner and Gallimore of Caughley, and Dillwyn at Swansea also produced thousands of pieces which included soapstone. All were part of the early English Industrial Revolution and are now equally studied and admired.

The Soapstone quarries have now almost been absorbed back into nature but the footprint they have left in the Mullion and Landewednack parishes is still visible. It should not be forgotten that they had a huge influence on the development of the early ceramic industry in Britain as well as providing employment to Cornish men and women and hundreds of people in the Porcelain trade throughout the Country. They still create thousands of pounds towards the economy by the beauty and quality of decoration and their rarity.

The cottage industry of turning and polishing soapstone and serpentine still clings on, but for how long?

By bringing the story of soaprock on the Lizard back into the public awareness it may be possible to give the quarries and the skills of the quarrymen and miners the recognition they undoubtedly deserve after almost 200 years in the wilderness. To be able to walk uninterrupted along one of the most attractive coastal paths in the Country, which is in effect another lost historical and industrial landscape perhaps we should stop and think of how life has changed in the last 250 years.

There are small pieces of the Industry and small pieces of a lost way of life still in existence and hopefully they can continue to be preserved, studied and understood. Through the perception of the Victorians who recognised the significance and quality of the Porcelain which graced royalty and the general public alike, collections were built and the soaprock porcelain displayed. Today we try to achieve the same in local Heritage centres around the country and as a result it is still possible to view many of the early pieces now sought after by hundreds of collectors throughout the world ... each piece containing a little bit of Cornwall's Soaprock Coast.

17. Appendix

Appendix 1

CONVERSION INFORMATION

Throughout the book measurements,weights and monetary values are given in the original form, and in order to bring these up to date a conversion table has been made available.

a) In 1266 the system of coinage took shape in this country under Henry II when it was decided that one penny should weigh the same amount as 32 grains of wheat, and 8 pounds would be the weight of a gallon of wine, thus establishing the link between money and weight. Currency values were in Guineas, pounds shillings and pennies and farthings. Guineas were minted in this country between 1663 and 1813 and made of gold. Their value changed with the value of gold resulting in changes to the weight and size of the coin. During the French Revolution and the Revolutionary wars people hoarded gold coins and in 1799 the production of guineas was halted. The government passed a law making bank notes legal tender in any amount. The last issue of Guineas was in 1813, and was to pay for the Duke of Wellingtons Campaign in the Pyrenees. In 1816 the guinea was replaced in currency by the pound and in coinage by the Sovereign. Until 1971 there were 240 pennies in a pound instead of 100 today, 8 crowns in a pound, 20 shillings in a pound, 12 pennies in a shilling, 24 halfpennies in a shilling, 4 farthings in a penny. Farthings were not used after 31st December 1960. Decimalisation was introduced in 1971 so the equivalent value of a guinea in decimal money is £1 and 5pence. With decimalisation a shillings became 5 new pence, sixpence became 2 and a half new pence and one new penny was the equivalent of 2.4 old pennies.

Examples One shilling became 5 new pence, Five shillings became 25 new pence,ten shillings 50 new pence, £8-5s-9d-3/4 is eight pounds five shillings and ninepence three farthings or £8.29p £8-9s-10d-1/4 is eight pounds nine shillings and ten pence farthing or £8.49p £32-12s-5d-2/4 is thirty two pounds twelve shillings and five pence halfpenny or £32.62p

b) Weights were measured in Tons, hundredweights and pounds., The British convention used weights of 16 (oz) ounces per pound (lb) 14 lbs per Stone, 8 Stones in a hundredweight (cwt), 4 quarters in a hundredweight, and 20 hundredweight in a Ton. There are 2240 lbs in a Ton. The weight of minerals was required to be given in tons and hundredweights.

Examples in the book include

10lbs = 4.53 Kg	1 cwt = 50.8.Kg 5cwt = 254.01 Kg) 10cwt = 508.02 Kg)
1 ton = 1.016 metric tons (1016Kg)	5 tons = 5.08 metric tons (5,080.2Kg)
10 tons = 10.16 metric tons (10,160.4Kg)	20 tons = 20.32 metric tons 20,320.98 Kg

c) Distances were measured in feet and inches, yards, chains,furlongs and miles. There were 12 inches to a foot, 3 feet per yard, 22 yards in a chain,10 chains in a furlong and 80 chains in a mile, 8 furlongs in a mile, and 1760 yards in a mile. The origin of such measurements goes back to Anglo Saxon times. An Anglo Saxon Field was the amount of land which could be ploughed by a team of oxen in a day. A furlong being the length of a plough furrow in a strip field system before the oxen were turned.

10 foot = 3.04metres	20 foot = 6.096 metres	30 foot = 9.144. metres	40 foot = 12.2 metres
50 foot = 15.24 metres	100 foot = 30.49 metres	200 foot = 60.96 metres	1 mile = 1.609 Km

d) Nautical Lengths were used in Mining terminology. A fathom was traditionally the length of a mans arm spread from fingertip to fingertip and approximates to 6 foot. Until 1949 the length of a section of anchor chain used in the Royal Navy was 12 and a half fathoms.

1 fathom = 6 foot = 1.83 metres   5 fathoms = 30 foot = 9.144. metres 10 fathoms = 60 foot = 18.28 metres. I hope you can "fathom" out the conversions, fathoms included water depths and were the origin of the phrase "to fathom something out" or ....getting to the bottom of it ! Source Wikipedia Conversion chart www.onlineconversion.com

Appendix 2

QUARTER DAYS

In Britain Quarter Days were the four traditional days when servants were hired and rents were due. They fell on four religious festivals roughly 3 months apart and close to the 2 solstices and 2 equinoxes. Their significance is now limited although leasehold payments and rents for business premises in England on the old Quarter Days. Quarter Days have been used since the Middle Ages and ensured that debts were not allowed to linger on. Accounts had to be settled , a reckoning had to be made and publicly recorded on the quarter days. In England they are a) Lady day 25th March, b) Midsummer Day 24th June, c) Michaelmas Day 29th September and d) Christmas Day 25th December. The Soapstone Licences issued in the 18th and 19th century by Landowners to potters were issued so that Rents commenced or were due on these days and default in payment would lead to suspension and revocation of any previously issued Licences. The Landowners also ensured that the Soapstone was weighed before it could be shipped in order to assess accounts correctly.

Appendix 3

In the 1970s the late John Penderill-Church was Historical Consultant for the ECC Quarry Group and had a great interest in the Lizard soapstone deposits and early British steatitic porcelain. He had a regular dialogue with people with similar interests and was keen to produce a documentary record of its history and development. In the course of his research he prepared but did not publish his results. These have been archived at Worcester Porcelain Museum for many years.In the course of researching this book I have been able to access some of his material. Some of his interpretations may now, in the light of subsequent research not be considered to be an entirely accurate representation, but with this in mind I have prepared a "List of Soapstone users" based on information obtained from several sources including some material from Penderill - Church.

Because there are no doubt a number of Licences still not within the public domain this list is produced as an appendix to this book in the hope that it can be developed in the future through ongoing academic investigation.

The locations shown within the licenses below relating to Mullion Cove/Predannack from 1772 are not entirely clear.

LIZARD SOAPROCK LICENCES 1748 TO 1828

Date	Location	Term/Expiry	Pottery	Landowner
1748*	Gew Graze	21 yrs to 1770	Lund/Miller Bristol	John West, Erisay (d.1758)
1751	Caerthillian Mill Kynance Cove (Caerthillian Crofts)	10 yrs to 1761	Crisp and John Sanders	Visc. Falmouth (Lambeth)
1751	Lizard Common Landwednack	10yrs to 1761	Crisp & John Sanders	Mary Hunt(Lanhydrock)
1752	Goon Vean/PorthPyg Pedenankea	10yrs to 1762	Crisp & Sanders	Mary Hunt(Lanhydrock)
1752	Gew Graze	Rem. 17yrs of Lund Lic.	Richard Holdship (Worcester)	
1756	Predannack Wartha Goss Moor/Wheal Providence	14 yrs to 1770	Richard Chaffers (Liverpool)	Visc. Falmouth
1757 *	Gew Graze... ownership of mineral rights passed to Visc. Falmouth			
1760	Caerthillian Crofts	10yrs to 1770	Badderley & Yates (Newcastle-u-lyne)	Visc Falmouth
1760	Daroose	10yrs to 1770	John Thorneloe (Worcester)	Visc Falmouth
1760	Gew Graze... Josiah Holdship took over Richard Holdships Worcester Licence			
1765	Predannack Downs	14 yrs to 1779	Phillip Christian and son Liverpool (successors to Chaffers)	Thomas Grylls, Helston
1770	Gew Graze Original lease expired... put up for sale and taken by John Nancarrow of Breage & Josiah Holdship of Worcester from Visc Falmouth 21yrs to 1791 Worcester			
1770	Daroose	21yrs to 1791	Worcester	John Hunt (Lanhydrock)
1770	Caerthillian Crofts	10yrs to 1781	Worcester	Visc Falmouth

(went on to sell mineral rights to Sir Christopher Hawkins,Trewithen)

1772	Mullion Cove/Predannack	21yrs to 1791	Phillip Christian (Liverpool)	
1773	Trethevas, Landwednack	7yrs to 1780	Philip Christian(Liverpool)	Thom. Fonnereau, Bochym
1775	Gew Graze… Worcester allowed their lease to run out as they believed ithe site had run out of soaprock.			
1775	Mullion Cove/Predannack	16yrs to 1791	Worcester remaining 16yrs of Christian lease taken over by Worcester	
1777	Meaver Vean	21yrs to 1798	Potters Soaprock Co (John Nicholas, John Lean, William Thomas (Mullion) Thomas Trounson (Mullion)	Visc Falmouth
1778	Predannack Downs	14 yrs to 1792	Thomas Turner, Ambrose Gallimore Royal Salopian Manuf, Caughley	Thomas Grylls and Peter Prisk
1780	Gew Graze	21yrs to 1801	Turner/Gallimore ,Caughley (Had hidden reserves)	
1780	Caerthillian Crofts	10yrs to 1790	Worcester	Sir Christopher Hawkins
1780	Lizard Common	10yrs to 1790	Worcester	Sir Christopher Hawkins
1783	Caerthillian Crofts ¬ Remainder of Worcester lease taken over by Thomas Flight of Worcester			
1790	Caerthillian Crofts	10yrs to 1800	Thomas Flight Worcester	
1792	Predannack Downs	14yrs to 1806	Turner	Caughley Grylls and Prisk
1799	Predannack Downs Remainder of Turner lease taken over by John Rose and Edward Blakeways of Coalport			
1800	Caerthillian Crofts	10yrs to 1810	Flight and Barr Worcester	
1801	Gew Graze 21yrs to 1822		Turner lease taken over Flight and Barr Worcester	
1810	Caerthillian Crofts	10yrs to 1820	Barr, Flight& Barr Worcester	
1814	Gew Graze 14yrs to 1828 setts adjacent to Flight and Barr taken out by Lewis Weston Dillwyn of Cambrian Pottery ,Swansea			
1853	Grade Parish	21yrs to 1874	Thomas Jackson, Pimlico	Rt.Hon. Evelyn Visc. Falmouth

Serpentine, Steatite Stone,Soapstone, Diallage ….. main use believed to be ornamental stone for Carving.

Appendix 4

Copy of Predannack Wartha Manor Court Book 1750 Source, Courtney Library, Truro. HU/13/8

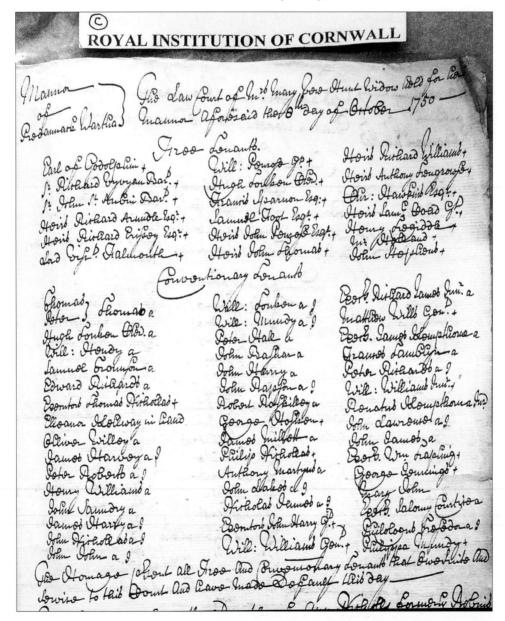

Appendix 5

Source

Morton - Nance E, "Soaprock Licences", English Ceramic Circle,1935 Cornwall Record Office, Truro.p.73-84. Ref FS/3/1104/5

COUNTERPART of Lease of Soapy Rock & Clays to Benjamin Lund for Twenty One Years at 10s. per Ton

THIS INDENTURE made the seventh day of March In the two & Twentyeth year of ye reign of our Sovereign Lord George the Second by ye Grace of God of Great Britain France Ireland King Defender of ye faith &c. And in the year of Our Lord One thousand seven hundred forty & eight BETWEEN John West of Bury Saint Edmonds in the County of Suffolck Esquire of the one part and Benjamin Lund of the City of Bristol Merchant of the other part WITNESSETH that for & in Consideration of ye payments reservations Covenants & Agreements hereinafter mentioned & Agreed on the part & behalf of the sd Benjamin Lund his Execs. Adms. & Assignes to be made done & performed He ye sd John West HATH Sett & Granted & by these presents doth Sett & Grant unto ye sd Benjamin Lund his Execs. Adms. & Assignes Liberty power Lycense and Authority to break up take & Carry away such parts & parcells as he and they shall think proper of all that Clay or Soft Rock Comonly Called or known by the Name of the Soapy Rock lying in Gewcrease Cove within that Tenement or Great Inclosure Called or known by the Name of Kinance in ye parish of Mullion in the County of Cornwall Aforesaid And also to dig & Search for ye Same or ye Like Clays or Rocks in & throughout those parts of the sd Tenement or Inclosure which now are or late were in ye tenure or Occupation of Barnard Richards Richard Sampson & James & John Harry or any or either of them their or any or either of their Undertenant or Undertenants & to raise break up take and Carry away ye same to & for his & their own Use & uses & at his or their own wills & pleasures (PROVIDED & so as ye sd Benjamin Lund . . . and all Workmen Labourers or others to be employed by or under him do as little damage as possible to ye sd Tenement . . .) TO HAVE HOLD USE Exercise & Enjoy ye sd Lycences Libertyes powers Authorityes & Premisses hereinbefore mentioned to be Sett or Granted or Intended So to be unto ye sd Benjamin Lund his Execs. Adms. & Assignes YIELDING & paying therefore during ye sd Terme unto ye sd John West his Heirs & Assignes for every Ton weight of the sd Clays or Rocks that Shall be broke up & Carried away from ye sd Tenement of Kinance aforesaid . . . ye Sume of Ten shillings of Lawfull money of Great Britain Clear of all Charges whatsoever & so proportionally for a Lesser part then a Ton . . . AND further also that ye sd Benjamin Lund . . . Shall & will permit and Suffer any person or persons who Shall be from time to time Appointed by ye sd John West . . . to be present at ye diging Searching breaking up weighing off & Carrying away ye sd Clays or Rocks & to take Accounts of ye Same And Shall & will well & duly give or Cause to be given unto ye sd John West . . . Six days Notice of every weighing & Carrying off ye sd Clays or Rocks to ye end that he . . . may be present at ye doing thereof AND Shall & will also within three months next ensuing ye date hereof at his . . . proper Costs & Charges begin to work in the Searching for raising & breaking up the sd

Clays or Rocks & Shall & will Yearly & every year of ye terme aforesaid So raise break up weigh off & carry away at Lest Twenty Tons of ye sd Clays or Rocks if so much Shall be found within ye Premises aforesaid AND Shall not nor will destroy rifle or render Useless or permit or Suffer to be destroyed rifled or rendered Useless any of ye fixed Timbers Boards or Stemples which Shall or may be placed or putt up for ye better Security or Support of ye Country in diging Searching or Sinking for the sd Clays or Rocks PROVIDED Nevertheless & it is ye true Intent & meaning of these presents & of ye partyes hereunto that if ye sd Benjamin Lund his Execs. Adms. or Assignes Shall not well & truly pay . . . unto ye sd John West . . . ye sd Clear Sume of Ten shillings for every Ton weight of ye sd Clays or Rocks which Shall be raised . . . Or shall not raise & Carry away at Lest Twenty Tons thereof in every Year . . . THEN & in either of these Cases this Grant or Sett shall be Null and Utterly void . . . AND ye sd John West doth for himself . . . Covenant promise & Grant unto & with ye sd Benjamin Lund . . . that ye sd Benjamin Lund . . . Shall or may quietly & peacably have hold possess & enjoy all & Singular ye Libertyes powers privileges & Authorityes aforesaid without Lawfull Lett Suit Trouble Molestation Disturbance aforesaid without Lawfull Lett Suit Trouble Molestation Disturbance or denyall whatsoever . . . IN WITNESS whereof ye partyes' abovesaid to these present Indentures their hands & Seales interchangeably have putt the day & year above written.

           [Seal]

[Signed] BENJN. LUND.

Sealed and Delivered (on treble—Sixpenny Stamp—parchment) by the within named Benjamin Lund in the presence of

           [Signed] JOHN LLOYD.
                 ANN OLIVER.

18. Bibliography

1. http://www.cornwallwildlifetrust.org.uk/nature_reserves/where_to_find_the_nature_reserves_1/map

2. http://www.genuki.org.uk/big/eng/Cornwall/Mullion/

3. http://www.historic-cornwall.org.uk/a2m/bronze_age/hc_settlement/kynance%20gate/kynance_gate.htm

4. Harvey, Rev. E.G. Mullyon: Its history, Scenery and Antiquities. 1875

4a. Borlase ,William Copeland   "Naenia Cornubiae" 1872

5. William Borlase "Natural History of Cornwall" p67-69, 1758 Available at Oxford Digital Library. http://www2.odl.ox.ac.uk

5a. Unpublished notes of John Penderill-Church Worcester Porcelain Museum Archives.

6. J.F. Berger Transactions of the Geol.Soc. Cornwall "Observations on Physical structure of Devonshire and Cornwall ,p130. 1811 Available at http://books.google.com

7. http://www.thepotteries.org/types/porcelain.htm

8. Exhibiton Pack compiled by Anna Dolecka, Education officer Worcester Museum & Art Gallery 1994.

9. Taken from W. Borlase, Lanisley letters. Jnl Royal Inst. Cornwall XXIII, 1753

10. www.smugglers.oldcornwall.org/smugglers.htm

11. Hamilton Jenkin. A. K. Cornwall & its people. 1933

12. www.tea.co.uk/east-india-company   United Kingdom Tea Council website.

13. http://royalsociety.org/about-us/history/

14. SITJARhttp://sitjar.sit.ac.nz/publications/Jno_Campbell_letter_and_the_Bow_manufactory.pdf

15. Brewster Sir David, The Edinburgh Encyclopedia First Pub. 1830 http://books.google.co.uk/books?

16. Nilson, Jan Erik. Letters of Pere d`Entrecolles. Gotheborg.com/letters/index.shtml

17. Sherwood M. Reamurs Road, New Scientist February 24th 1983. http://books.google.co.uk/books?

18. As 5.

19. Emanuel Mendes da Costa. A natural History of fossils 1757.

19a. Spero S. Lunds Bristol and Early Worcester Porcelain. 1750-1758. 2006

20. http://www.hrionline.ac.uk/conisbrough/find/manor_court.html

20a. As 5.

20b. Predannack Manor Court Book. Courtney Library, Truro. HU/13/8

20c. Fortescue Hitchins , The History of Cornwall from the earliest Records & Traditions.Vol 2 1824 Edited by Samuel Drew. Available at http://books.google.com/books

20d. www.spreadthetruth.co.uk/Articles/Wesley.html

20e. http://legal-dictionary.com/manorial

21. As 11. Cornish Homes and Customs; The Cottage Home

22. http://www.cornishhedges.co.uk/PDF/roadside.pdf   Copyright Robin Meneer 2008

23. As 11. The Western Land.

24. Map J. Polsue. Lakes Parochial History of Cornwall 1867. Sourced 1st Edition as 4.(Harvey)

25. West Briton Cornish Newspaper 1836 http://west-penwith.org.uk/wb1836.htm

26. http://www.archive.org/stream/oldfalmouth00gays/oldfalmouth Susan E. Gay "Old Falmouth" 1903

27. http://smugglers.oldcornwall.org/contents.htm The Federation of Old Cornwall Societies.

28. Osler, Edward The Life of Admiral Viscount Falmouth 1835 http://books.google.com/books

29. As 4 Rambles through the Parish.

30. Morton - Nance E, "Soaprock Licences", English Ceramic Circle,1935 Cornwall Record Office, Truro. p.73-84. Ref FS/3/1104/5

30a. Parkinson Dr Sonia G., Soaprock Licences Research Report Part 1 Crisp and Sanders, Badderley and Yates, Chaffers NCS Newsletter 92, 1993

30b. Parkinson Dr Sonia G., Soaprock Licences Research Report Part 2 NCS Newsletter 93, 1994

31. As 5a. Letters

32. Pococke Richard, Dr. The Travels through England Vol. Printed for the Camden Society. 1888 http://www.archive.org/stream/travelsthroengland00camduoft#page/120/mode/2up

33. Watney B. The Lizard. A Magazine of Field Studies. New Series Vol1 no 2 "Soapy Rock and its connection with pottery" 1958

34. As 5.

35. http://www.cornwall-calling.co.uk/mines/slate/tintagel.htm

36. Charleston R.J. & Mallett JVG A problematical group of 18th Century porcelains. Account book at Courtney Library Truro.

36a www.cornwalls.co.uk/Penzance/history.htm

36b. www.northwag.org

37. Dawson Aileen . The Art of Worcester porcelain. 1751-1788. 2008 http://books.google.co.uk

38. Binns Richard. A century of Potting in the City of Worcester. 1865

38a. Green,Valentine. A survey of the City of Worcester 1764 http://books.google.co.uk/books

39. www.antique-marks.com/antique-english-porcelain.html.

39a. VAUXHALL_AND_BOVEY_TRACEY_CHRONOLOGY

40. Chaffers, W. "Marks and Monograms on Porcelain and Pottery" 1874 http://www.archive.org/stream/marksmonogramson00chaf#page/686/mode/2up

41. Cunnack, Richard J. "Cunnack Manuscript" Notes on mines bewteen 1845-1908 Ed. Justin Brooke. Courtesy of The Trevithick Society.

42. Landydrock Agents Rough Book at Courtney Library Truro.

42a. Hamilton Jenkin, A.K.. Mines and Miners of Cornwall. Vol XIII

43. Paris, J. Royal. Geol. Soc. Cornwall Vol1 1818" On accidents which occur in the mines of Cornwall .... http://books.google.com

43a. http://www.geevor.com/

43b. http://www.trevarno.co.uk/about-trevarno/history.htm

44. Geophysical Research letters Vol 35 2008 https://2027293623233439848-a-glaciology-net-s-sites.googlegroups.com/a/glaciology.net/grinsted/Home/PDFs/jevrejeva

44a. www.bgs.ac.uk/research/earthquakes/British Tsunami.html

45. Johns C.A., Rev. A week at the Lizard. 1848

46. As 42a

47. Encyclopaedia of geomorphology, Vol 2 Andrew Gouldie 2004

48. As 41.

49. e-mail from Prof. C. Bristow. Exeter 12.5.11

50. Burt R. Short Hist. of British Mining technology in the 18th/19th Centuries 1982

51. Sublevel stoping. C Haycocks & RC Aelick MSE Mining Engineering Handbook

52. Mullion Tithe Map and Apportionments. 1841 Cornwall Record Office Truro

53. ditto

54. Josiah Wedgwood Common Place Book 1

54a. Parkinson Dr. Sonia F.G. Soaprock Licences before Research Report part 3, NCS newsletter 94 June 1994

55. As 52

56. www.british-history.ac.uk/report.aspx?compid=22873   British History Online

57. www.encyclo.co.uk/define/willow-pattern

58. Turner Soapstone Indenture Ref DD RH 1388 Cornwall Record Office Truro

59. As 38.

60. Binns Richard W. A century of Potting in the City of Worcester. 1865 List of Worcester Directors

61. Warner, Richard Rev. " A Tour through Cornwall in the Autumn of 1808"

62. Smith B.P. "A trip to the Far West " 1840

63. As 45

64. As 46

65. http://www.nantgarwandswanseaporcelain.co.uk/

66. http://www.cornwall-calling.co.uk/famous-cornish-people/cookworthy.htm

67. http://www.worcesterporcelainmuseum.org.uk/

68. http://www.google.co.uk/intl/en_uk/earth/

69. Predannack Wartha Manor Court Book, Courtney Library, Truro Ref. HU/13/8

Bibliography - Additional References

The following list of references may add to the readers knowledge of the subject.

R.W. Binns "A guide through the Royal Worcester Porcelain Works" 1883

Harry Carter "The autobiography of a Cornish smuggler" 1900

Rose, Kerr & Nigel Wood "Science and Civilisation in China"

William Penaluna "The Crcle or Historical Survey of 60 Parishes & Towns in Cornwall" 1819

Abraham Rees "The cyclopaedia or Universal dictionary of arts, sciences" Vol.34 1819

www.kalendar.demon.co.uk/porcelain.htm   Lunds Bristol soft paste porcelain

www.haughton.com/richardburt   "The origins of Worcester Porcelain 1740-1751"

www.stokemuseums.org.uk

www.kalendardemon.co.uk/delfbrisredcliff.htm   More on Redcliff Backs, Bristol

http://sitjar.sit.ac.nz/publications/Jno   Campbell letter and the Bow manufactory.pdf

www.jstor.org/pss/25616645   J.V. Owen "On the earliest products of the Worcester Porcelain manufactory Vol.32 No.4

www.northwag.org/joomladev   Astley Forge Mill Soapstone Mill for Worcester

www.darwincountry.org/explore/000542.html   Caughley Porcelain

www.britainexpress.com/History/tea-in-britain.htm   The History of tea in Britain

www.archive.org/stream/abcofenglishsalt00blacuoft/abcofenglishsalt00blacuoft_djvu.txt
         The ABC of English salt glaze stoneware. From Dwight to Doulton

www.museumwales.ac.uk/en/105   Morton Nance collection of Welsh Pottery and Porceslains

www.clayheritage.org/pages/history(1).htm   The history of ball clay production

         ... and, of course, Wikipedia.org

"This book is dedicated to our parents"

RF